COOK TO INSPIRE

PRYOR PUBLICATIONS

MEMBER OF
INDEPENDENT PUBLISHERS GUILD

75 Dargate Road, Yorkletts, Whitstable,
Kent CT5 3AE, England.

Tel. & Fax: (01227) 274655

Specialist in Facsimile Reproductions.

Published by Pryor Publications
for
INSPIRE

Regd. Charity No. 296284

Compiled by Vanessa Cumberlege
Illustrated by Anne Koska

ISBN 0946014 46 9

A CIP Record for this book is available from the British Library.

Typeset by Paul Hanks in 10pt/11pt Goudy Oldstyle
172 Dargate Road, Yorkletts, Whitstable, Kent CT5 3AH
Tel. & Fax: (01227) 262735

Printed and Bound by
Biddles Ltd.

Woodbridge Park Estate,
Woodbridge Road,
Guildford GU1 1DA

In December 1992, whilst I was working in France as a cook, I slipped on some ice and fell 15 feet, dislocating and fracturing my lower back and bruising my spinal cord.

I spent 5 months in the spinal unit at Salisbury District Hospital and gradually learnt to walk again after initial paralysis. Constant visits from my family and friends kept my spirits high and gave me the determination, inspiration and motivation to battle on. I shall forever be grateful and words cannot ever thank everyone enough for all they did for me.

My eyes have certainly been opened to the world of those with spinal injuries and the enormous difficulties faced with day to day living. This little book is my effort to raise money for the charity, INSPIRE, which is understandably so close to my heart.

"Cook to INSPIRE" may not rival Delia Smith in your kitchen but it is great fun and filled with the favourite recipes of both friends and famous people.

Julie Gardner from INSPIRE has been amazing on the computer and most of the credit has to go to her, but above all my thanks must go to my parents and brother for all their love and support.

I hope you enjoy this book as much as I've enjoyed compiling it. Happy cooking!

Vanessa Cumberlege

Vanessa Cumberlege

Royalties from this publication will go to INSPIRE.

THE INTEGRATED SPINAL REHABILITATION FOUNDATION "INSPIRE"

INSPIRE was founded by persons who themselves had suffered the effects of spinal cord injuries. Their idea was to fund programmes of medical, mechanical or electronic nature, conducted with the express intent of providing practical aid to persons who had suffered similarly.

In the past year INSPIRE has been part of a team the work of which has enabled persons who have broken their necks to regain the use of their hands. The funds raised in this period have been used in part to purchase a system, known as "Freehand," from a medical team in the United States. The first recipient of this system is able, for the first time since his accident some fourteen years ago, to use his previously totally paralysed hand to perform all of the day to day tasks that most of us, perhaps understandably, take for granted.

Perhaps as many as 7000 persons who have broken their necks, and hence lost the use of their arms and legs, are living around the British Isles and we know that a goodly portion of them could, given the availability of adequate funding, be helped to regain functional use of their hands and in so doing gain a measure of self esteem brought about by the outcome of the work INSPIRE is funding. To that 7000 must be added another 8–9000 persons who have broken their backs — these paraplegics also need the help of INSPIRE.

It is thanks to the likes of Nessie, and the funds she hopes to raise from the sales of her cookbook, that INSPIRE is able to offer financial support to those medical and bio–engineering personnel whose unique talents make possible the improvements in the lives of those who are spinally injured.

Jack Gardner
Executive Director
INSPIRE

The INSPIRE Foundation, Duke of Cornwall Spinal Treatment Centre,
Salisbury District Hospital, Wiltshire, SP2 8BJ. Tel: 01722 336262 ext 2465

CONTENTS

Pages

1. STARTERS 7
2. SOUPS 19
3. FISH 29
4. MAIN COURSE:
   - BEEF 36
   - CHICKEN 39
   - GAME 50
   - LAMB 55
   - LIVER 58
   - PASTA 60
   - PORK 66
5. VEGETARIAN 71
6. THIS & THAT 83
7. PUDDINGS 93
8. ICE CREAMS 109
9. TEA TIME 113

STARTERS

ITALIAN ANTIPASTA

Amanda Carr, *London*

Ingredients:

Serves 4

1 yellow pepper
3 small red onions
shavings of parmesan cheese
6–8 oz mozzarella
1 oz pinenuts (toasted)
4 flat parsley sprigs OR
basil leaves to decorate

1 red pepper
20 roquette leaves
slices parma ham
olive oil
ground pepper & salt
balsamic vinegar
butter

Method:

Cut the peppers in half and scoop out the seeds, place on a baking tin, brush with olive oil and roast in a hot oven until skin blisters, allow to cool, then peel and cut the onions into quarters and pan–fry in butter until caramelised and soft.

Slice the mozzarella into 8 portions. Arrange the ingredients attractively on dinner plates in little piles. Sprinkle the roquette with the roasted pinenuts and put the parmesan shavings on the top. Just before serving, sprinkle with balsamic vinegar.

Comment: Easy summer starter.

BASIL & TOMATO SOUFFLE

Sarah Wills, *Director Blues Cookery Agency, London*

Ingredients: **Serves 4**

2 oz butter/margarine
2 oz gruyère cheese
1 oz emmental cheese
3 level tsp sundried tomato paste
salt and pepper
2 oz flour
½ pt milk
4 eggs
1 tbsp (heaped) fresh chopped basil
grated parmesan

Method:

Set oven to 200C, 400F or Gas Mark 6. Brush a heat proof bowl or 6 inch soufflé dish with melted butter. Melt butter in a heavy-bottomed saucepan, pour in flour and cook for a minute stirring all the time and add milk gradually, stir over the heat while the mixture comes to the boil. It will be a very thick paste and is ready when the mixture leaves the sides of the pan as you stir it. Remove from the heat and allow to cool slightly, stir in cheese, seasoning, tomato paste and chopped basil.

Separate eggs and beat yolks into the mixture one at a time. In a large bowl whisk the egg whites until soft but not dry, beat a spoonful of whites into the soufflé mixture. Using a large metal spoon carefully fold into the mixture, making sure not to over mix. Turn into the buttered dish, sprinkle with parmesan. Bake for approx 20 minutes — it is ready when the mixture remains fairly steady.

Comment: This soufflé is delicious served with a roquette salad and hot focaccia bread as a lunch dish.

CHALET CHEESE SOUFFLES

Sarah Sutherland–Pilch, *Event & Conference Organiser in London*

Ingredients:

Makes 10 Ramekins

3 oz butter
3 oz flour
9 oz strong cheddar/gruyère
pinch of nutmeg

¾ pt of milk
1 good tsp mustard
6 eggs, separated
salt and pepper

Sauce:

button mushrooms, lightly cooked

¾ pt single cream

Method:

Grease inside of 10 ramekins. Melt butter and add flour and mustard, cook for 2-3 minutes. Add milk, salt, pepper and nutmeg and bring sauce to the boil stirring all the time. When thick leave to cool, and then add grated cheese. Add egg yolks and check seasoning.

Whisk egg whites until stiff and then fold into cheese sauce. Transfer into ramekins and cook in a bain-marie for 15-20 minutes in a medium hot oven until well risen and golden. Leave to cool and sink (if you're in the Alps go skiing!) Turn out into greased serving dish, pour over some cream and lightly fried mushrooms then reheat for 15 minutes.

Comment: It is the only soufflé guaranteed to rise at altitude and allows you to ski all day without it sinking!

CHICKEN LIVER PATE

Mrs Kitty Wilson, *Sissinghurst*

Ingredients: **Serves 4**

½ lb chicken livers
2 tsp onion juice
1 tsp salt & dash of cayenne pepper
½ tin consommé
1 tbsp gelatine
sprinkle of nutmeg or mace
⅛ tsp ground cloves
1 tsp mustard
¼ lb butter
3 tbsp port
dash of Angostura bitters

Method:

Simmer chicken livers until tender (approx. 20 minutes), then drain and put through mincer or blender while still hot. Add softened butter and spices and beat in a mixer until smooth and fluffy. Add onion juice and 1 tbsp of port and beat a little more.

Jelly: Heat consommé, add gelatine, 1-2 tbsps port, dash of Angostura bitters. Put a layer of this in the bottom of the container you are going to use and set it in the freezer. Then press the liver mixture on top and cover with another layer of the consommé mixture.

Comment: This keeps well in the fridge for at least a week so can be made well ahead of time for a party. Serve as a starter or on small biscuits with drinks.

INSALATA DEL FUNGI

Mrs Pam Carling, *Clapham, London*

Ingredients:

Serves 4

8 oz mushrooms
1 lemon (juice)
3 cloves of garlic
1 tsp sugar
¼ pt double cream
6 oz prawns
6 shakes of tabasco
salt and pepper
olive oil
parsley

Method:

Slice the mushrooms and saturate in olive oil. Stir in lemon juice, garlic and seasonings. Chill in fridge for 1 hour or overnight. Stir in cream and prawns. To serve, sprinkle with lots of parsley.

Comment: Make sure your sleeping partner has some too!

LAYERED SARDINE PATE

Mrs Polly Preston, *Thornthorpe, N. Yorkshire*

Ingredients: **Serves 6**

4 oz butter
2 tins sardines
2–3 cloves of garlic—crushed
a big handful of chopped parsley
1 lb cream cheese
½ lemon (juice only)
1 small brown loaf, thinly sliced
salt & black pepper

Method:

Butter a loaf tin. Melt 3 oz butter and leave it to cool a bit. Mash sardines in a bowl with cream cheese, add lemon juice, garlic and melted butter gradually and add salt and pepper to taste.

Mix thoroughly. Melt remaining butter (you may need a bit extra) and stir the chopped parsley into it. Spread this mixture on the bottom of the loaf tin. Cut crusts off the slices of bread and cut to shape to make a layer of bread on top of the parsley mixture.

Spread a thick layer of the cream cheese mixture over the bread, then another layer of bread, and so on, ending with a layer of bread on the top. Cover with foil and chill overnight in the fridge.

Comment: This is a very good and unusual pâté. It freezes extremely well and its dark green parsley butter top makes it look impressive!

MAGIC MUSHROOMS

Sallie Taylor, *Germany*

Ingredients:

Serves 4

1 lb button or chopped mushrooms
8 oz can tomatoes, with the juice
½ lemon, very thinly sliced
½ tbsp Grandpa's Chilli Sherry
1 tbsp coarsely crushed coriander seeds
4 tbsp olive oil
½ tbsp sherry vinegar
1 tbsp chopped fresh coriander
salt and black pepper

Grandpa's Chilli Sherry:

Green or red chillies
Sherry — dry, medium or sweet

Method:

(Fill a bottle with fresh chillies, pour the sherry over them and cork securely. Keep for 2–3 weeks before removing the chillies by decanting the sherry into other bottles).

Wash and dry mushrooms. Heat oil, vinegar and Grandpa's Chilli Sherry in a pan with coriander seeds. When hot, add everything else and cook furiously for 3–4 minutes. Scoop out the mushrooms and boil sauce rapidly to reduce by half. Pour sauce back over mushrooms. Cover, chill — eat when well chilled — it's well worth the wait!

Comment: Forget Worcestershire sauce, look no further than Grandpa's Chilli Sherry! Keeps indefinitely — a few drops are excellent in sauces, soups and salad dressings.

PÂTÉ EN CROUTE

Mrs Paddy Ashdown, *Somerset*

Ingredients:

Serves 6

8 oz chicken livers
1 crushed clove of garlic
1 tbsp chopped parsley
1 beaten egg
beaten eggs to glaze
pinch of mixed herbs
8 oz sausage meat
1 small chopped onion
8 oz streaky bacon
13 oz puff pastry
salt and freshly ground pepper

Method:

Chop chicken livers and put in a bowl with sausage meat, chopped onion, garlic, herbs, parsley, egg and seasoning and mix thoroughly. Remove rind from bacon and stretch with a knife. Grease a 1 lb loaf tin and line it with bacon — leaving 3 or 4 rashers for the top. Fill tin with chicken liver pâté and cover with remaining rashers and then tin foil. Put the tin in a bain marie (roasting tin with water) and cook 160C/Gas Mark 3 for 1½ hours. Cool completely and turn out.

Roll out pastry to a shape to take the pâté. Brush pâté with beaten eggs and place on pastry and wrap pâté in the pastry. Seal the edges well and brush the whole thing with the beaten eggs. Decorate with leaves etc made from the pastry trimmings and glaze these too.

Bake at 180C/Gas Mark 4 for approximately 30 minutes — until pastry is golden brown and well risen. Serve cold — smashing with toast and a tomato and basil salad.

Comment: I'm always asked where I buy this particular pâté! I suppose it's meant as a compliment!

SMOKED SALMON AND NOODLES

Sue Lawley, *TV Presenter*

Ingredients: **Serves 4**

4 oz sliced smoked salmon
2 oz freshly grated parmesan
1 dessertspoon chopped dill
  and fresh parsley
  a little grated nutmeg
6 fl oz double cream
1 pkt egg noodles
  (Angel Hair)
  salt and pepper

Method:

Cut the smoked salmon into thin strips. In a double saucepan reduce double cream stirring continuously and fold in cheese and nutmeg. Cook noodles in boiling water and drain. Add smoked salmon into the cream mixture then add the noodles and mix well. Serve with parsley and dill.

Comment: This recipe makes a succulent first course.

HOT SPINACH CHEESECAKE

Mrs Amanda Kay, *Indian Textile Importer*

Ingredients: **Serves 6**

2 oz butter
1 cup crushed cheese biscuits
¼ cup grated parmesan cheese
8 oz cream cheese
10½ oz sour cream
2 bunches spinach
1 medium onion, chopped
3 bacon rashers, chopped
4½ oz feta cheese
4 eggs, lightly beaten

Method:

Melt butter in saucepan. Add biscuit crumbs. Press evenly over base of greased flan dish. Put in fridge for 30 minutes. Cook spinach, drain and press out excess liquid and chop roughly. Cook bacon and onion stirring constantly until onion is soft. Beat cream cheese until smooth. Add parmesan, sour cream and eggs. Beat until all is combined. Stir in spinach and bacon/onion mixture. Pour this filling over base. Stand on oven tray and bake in moderate slow oven for 1 hour or until golden brown and set. Sprinkle with a bit more cheese and stand for 10 minutes before cutting.

Comment: Leave out the bacon and it becomes a dish for vegetarians!

NOTES

SOUPS

ARTICHOKE SOUP

Mrs Belinda Evans, *Kensington, London*

Ingredients:

Serves 6–8

2 lb Jerusalem artichokes
1 onion
½ glass white wine
salt and pepper
½ cucumber
¼ pint cream
stock

Method:

Peel and put the artichokes into a pan with enough stock to cover, along with the cucumber, and chopped onion. Cook until tender and liquidise. Season and add the wine and cream.

Comment: Serve with chopped chives — blob of cream and piping hot garlic bread. Fearfully quick, except for peeling of the artichokes.

ICED CARROT AND ORANGE SOUP

Mrs Maureen Shepheard, *Nr Colchester*

Ingredients:

Serves 4

1 lb carrots
1 onion
1 level tsp sugar
¼ pt of single cream
1½ pts chicken stock
1 oz butter
juice of 4 oranges

Method:

Soften the carrots and onion in the butter. Stir in sugar, stock and salt — cover and simmer gently. Put in liquidiser, add orange juice and cream. Put in fridge until very cold.

Comment: Delicious on a hot summer evening.

LEEK AND POTATO SOUP

Mrs Glenys Kinnock, *Member of the European Parliament*

Ingredients: **Serves 6**

4 large leeks
1 oz butter
freshly milled pepper
2–3 tbsp single cream (opt)
1 large potato
1½ pts chicken stock
salt

Method:

Trim green tops of leeks to about 1 inch of the white part and cut away base. Cut leeks lengthwise through to the centre and wash well in cold water. Shred leeks finely. Peel and cut potato into large dice-size pieces.

Melt butter in a saucepan and add leeks and potatoes. Cover and cook over a low heat until vegetables are soft. Stir in stock and bring up to the boil. Cover and simmer gently for about 30 minutes. Liquidize in a blender or pass through a sieve, half at a time. Season in the saucepan and stir in cream just before serving.

Comment: A very tasty and easy to make soup.

LENTIL SOUPERB

Moya Anchizi, *New York*, NY

Ingredients:

Serves 4

1 lb of lentils
2 large tomatoes, fresh or tinned
4 rashers of bacon, chopped (opt.)
2 qts water
1 tbsp parmesan cheese
3 peeled cloves of garlic
1 tbsp olive oil
1 soup cube, chicken/beef
top 3 or 4 inches of a head of celery (leaves and all) chopped

Method:

Fry the bacon in a large saucepan. Add rinsed lentils, water and other ingredients. Bring slowly to the boil and simmer for approximately one and a half hours or until the lentils are as soft as you wish to have them for a soup. If too thick add more water.

Taste and adjust seasoning. Stir from time to time to avoid sticking.

Comment: Do not serve this soup piping hot, but do add a tbsp of parmesan cheese and mix in. Each person should dribble some good olive oil into his bowl of soup.

QUICK ONION SOUP

Fiona Stally, *Putney*

Ingredients:

Serves 2

½ tbsp oil
2 large onions, finely sliced
3½ fl oz not-too-dry white wine
2½ oz good gruyere or emmental cheese, grated
sea salt & freshly ground black pepper
1 oz butter
14 fl oz vegetable or chicken stock
6 small slices of baguette-style bread

Method:

In a pan, heat oil over a moderate heat, add butter, swirl it round as it melts, then tip in onion. Turn up heat. Season lightly and saute for a few minutes, stirring frequently, until the onion is golden brown. Pour in stock and wine and bring to the boil. Reduce heat and cover. Simmer for at least 12 minutes — a little longer if time allows.

Meanwhile, preheat the grill to high and spread the grated cheese over the slices of bread. Season with pepper and grill until golden brown. Divide the cooked onion between 2 flameproof bowls, pour the soup into them and top with the prepared bread, cheese side up.

Comment: This is my favourite starter!! It is very filling so it makes a good light meal as well.

STILTON AND VEGETABLE SOUP

Sue Cook, *TV Presenter*

Ingredients:

Serves 4

2–3 large onions, chopped
½ pt milk or more, for creamier soup
season to taste
5 oz Stilton cheese
any uncooked vegetables (cauliflower, broccoli, leeks, etc.)

Method:

Peel and chop vegetables and cook them in a large saucepan. Don't throw away the water. Chop and fry onions until soft. Purée cooked vegetables and onions until smooth. Return mixture to the large saucepan containing the vegetable water and bring gently to the boil, stirring often. Add milk and crumble the cheese into the soup. Simmer until the cheese has dissolved. Season to taste.

Comment: Add a dash of cream, garnish with chives or sprinkle on some croutons. Serve with some hot garlic bread (if you can bear to wait any longer!)

PAM'S TOMATO SOUP

Mrs Pam Lytle, *Abbotts Ann, Wilts*

Ingredients:

Serves 3–4

8 oz chopped onions
2 oz cornflour
4 oz rindless streaky bacon
2 lbs tomatoes, skinned
 and roughly chopped
 finely grated nutmeg

2 oz butter
½ pt good chicken stock
1 can of tomato purée
1 tsp sugar
 salt and pepper
 bay leaf

Method:

Melt butter, fry bacon for a couple of minutes then add tomatoes and chopped onions. Cover and cook for 5 minutes stirring occasionally. Add sugar, pepper, chicken stock and bay leaf. Cover and cook for 30 minutes. Remove bay leaf and put all the ingredients into the Magimix. Strain through a sieve and add cornflour mixed in a little water. Simmer for a couple of minutes to thicken and add grated nutmeg and salt to taste.

Comment: Freezes really well and is much better than Heinz 57!!

TUSCAN BEAN SOUP

Mrs Mak Roberts, *London*

Ingredients:

Serves 6

12 oz cannelloni beans OR
white haricot beans
2 or 3 plump cloves of
garlic, crushed
lemon juice
1 tsp dried sage OR
couple of bay leaves
2 big handfuls of
chopped parsley
salt

Method:

Soak the beans overnight. Drain, then an hour or two before the soup is to be made, simmer them in two and a half pints of fresh water to which you have added the dried sage or bayleaves and a tablespoon of olive oil. Do not add salt at this stage.

When the beans are mushy, sieve or liquidize up to half of them and return to the saucepan to heat. Now pour the whole lot into a tureen or bowl from which you intend to serve the soup.

Keep it hot while you heat the parsley and garlic in good olive oil in a frying pan. Add this mixture to the waiting soup, add salt and lemon juice to taste and finish with a ladleful of the best olive oil you can afford.

Comment: This delightful soup is the authentic Italian Tuscan bean soup — just like momma used to make! It could not be simpler to make and requires no meat stock, yet has the thick and gelatinous qualities most welcome during the cold winter months.

WATERCRESS SOUP

H.R.H. The Princess of Wales, *Kensington Palace*

Ingredients: **Serves 6**

2 oz butter
2 pints chicken stock
1 pint single cream
2 oz flour
4 bunches of fresh watercress

Method:

Melt the butter, add flour and cook for a couple of minutes on a low heat, stirring gently. Slowly add warmed chicken stock until you have a creamy consistency. Wash the watercress thoroughly and add to the mixture. Cook slowly until the stalks are soft, stirring occasionally. This will take about 20 minutes. Remove from heat and allow to cool. Liquidise the soup and pass through a fine sieve. Chill and add the cream. Reserve a little of the cream to garnish the top of each portion.

Comment: A few leaves of watercress, previously blanched, can provide additional garnish.

NOTES

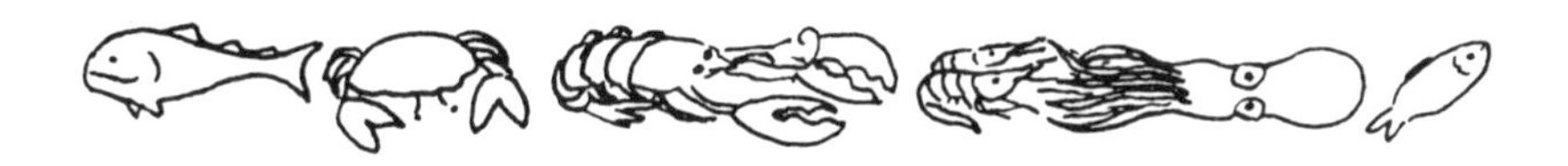

FISH

FISH STEAK CASSEROLE

Mrs Helen Wright, *Westbury, Wiltshire*

Ingredients:

Serves 4–6

2lb fish steaks (salmon, cod etc)
½ cup soured cream
1½ tsp lemon juice/lime juice
½ cup cheddar cheese, optional
can use breadcrumbs
½ cup mayonnaise
2 tsp flour
1 tbsp minced onion
cayenne pepper, to taste

Method:

Pour all ingredients mixed together over fish steaks. Bake in a hot oven for 20 minutes. Sprinkle with breadcrumbs or cheese and bake a further 2 minutes.

Comment: This wonderful recipe can be made in advance and cooked at the last minute. It mystifies all the best cooks and came, needless to say, out of a Californian cook book.

HADDOCK MONTE CARLO

Nicola Cox, *Cookery Writer*

Ingredients: **Serves 4–6**

1–1½ lb smoked haddock fillets
pepper to taste

½ lb tomatoes

Sauce:

1 oz butter
¼ pint milk
2-3 oz gruyère cheese, grated
salt, pepper and mace

1 oz flour
¼ pt whipping or
single cream

Method:

Skin haddock fillets and lay in one layer in a well buttered shallow baking dish. Skin, de-seed and dice tomatoes and scatter over fish. Season with pepper only. Pour sauce over and sprinkle with grated cheese. Bake uncovered in a moderately hot oven 375F/190C/Gas 5 for about 20 minutes. Brown under the grill if necessary.

Sauce:
Melt butter, add flour and cook for 2–3 minutes over moderate heat, stirring. Remove from the stove, wait for the sizzling to cease and add milk and cream. Bring to the boil, whisking with a wire whisk, and simmer for 1–2 minutes. Season with pepper, mace and very little salt. It should be a fairly thick coating sauce as some moisture will come out of the fish in the cooking.

Comment: This quick, delicious dish is from my book.

PRAWN BHOONA

Mrs Vicki Bays, *East Woodlands, Somerset*

Ingredients: **Serves 4**

1 cinnamon stick
½ tsp chilli powder
1 tsp turmeric
6 tbsp oil
fresh coriander
1 onion, chopped
4 fresh tomatoes, chopped
1 tsp garam masala
1 tsp ground cumin
2 tbsp tomato purée
1 bay leaf
1 lb prawns
2–3 garlic cloves
4–6 mushrooms

Method:

Heat oil and add cinnamon, bay leaf, onion and garlic — cook gently until soft. Add chopped tomatoes and mushrooms with spices and tomato purée. Add prawns and chopped coriander and season to taste with some salt and pepper.

Serving: Serve with rice.

Comment: Friends will think you cheated and bought this Bhoona from your local Tandoori Take–Away. It's so good, yum!

SALMON STEAKS WITH AVOCADO BUTTER

Mrs Pat Fordyce, *Stellenbosch, Sth Africa*

Ingredients: **Serves 6**

6 salmon steaks
1 tsp Worcestershire sauce
1 tbsp + 1 tsp lemon juice
¼ cup mashed avocado
1 tbsp chopped parsley
½ cup softened butter

Marinade:

3 tbsp lemon juice
½ tsp each basil and marjoram
½ tsp salt
1 cup cooking oil
½ tsp of garlic salt
½ tsp barbecue spice

Method:

Put marinade in a jar — cooking oil, ½ teaspoon of barbecue spice, 3 tablespoons of lemon juice, basil, pepper, marjoram, and salt — cover and shake well.

Place fish in a baking dish, pour over the marinade, cover and chill well. Leave for 4 hours or do it when you go to work in the morning, it won't hurt. Drain half the marinade from the fish and set it aside. Grill the fish for 4 minutes (2 inches from the heat). Turn steaks, spoon on remaining marinade and grill for a further 4 minutes or until cooked.

Avocado Butter:

Whip the butter until light and fluffy and fold in remaining ingredients. Cover and refrigerate until ready to use.

Serving: Transfer cooked steaks to a serving dish, top each with a knob of the butter and serve the rest in a bowl.

Comment: Very delicious and very glamorous and even yummier cooked on the barbie!

SPICY PRAWNS WITH COUSCOUS SALAD

Anton Mosimann, *Famous Swiss Chef*

Ingredients: **Serves 5**

12 fl oz vegetable OR chicken stock
1 tbsp black bean paste
2–3 oz pine kernels
3½ fl oz + 1 tbsp olive oil
1½ oz butter
3 oz seedless raisins, softened in warm water and drained
2 lemons, juice only
1 bunch spring onions, finely sliced
4 oz celery, finely sliced
3/4 oz saffron threads, infused in warm stock (2 tbsp)
pinch of ground cinnamon
½ oz fresh parsley, chopped
½ oz coriander, chopped
9 oz couscous
8 large prawns
coriander sprigs to garnish
seasoning

Method:

Melt butter in a pan and add the saffron liquid with the chicken or vegetable stock. Bring to the boil, then stir in couscous. Cover and remove the pan from the heat. Set aside for about 8 minutes until liquid is absorbed. Transfer to a bowl and fluff up grains with a fork. Add the celery, raisins, spring onions, parsley, coriander and pine kernels. Mix gently and leave to stand, uncovered.

Mix together in a bowl the lemon juice, cinnamon and seasoning. Whisk in 3½ fl oz of the oil until blended. Pour over couscous, toss and check seasoning.

Shell the prawns, split in half lengthways and de-vein. Season with salt and freshly ground black pepper. Heat remaining oil in a frying pan and sauté prawns for about 2 minutes. Stir in the black bean paste and cook for a few more seconds.

Serving: Arrange prawns over couscous and garnish with coriander sprigs.

Comment: Guaranteed compliments!

MAIN COURSE

FILLET STEAK ROYALE

Mrs Helen Saunders, *Wife of former Aston Villa striker, Dean — now at Galatasaray, Turkey*

Ingredients: **Serves 4**

4 fillet steaks
1 onion, chopped
8 fl oz white wine
2 tsp French mustard
1 clove garlic
4 tbsp olive oil
6 oz mushrooms, sliced
5 fl oz double cream
2 tbsp chopped fresh tarragon
salt & pepper

Method:

Flatten steak with a mallet. Heat oil in a pan, fry steaks turning regularly according to taste and put to one side. In another pan heat remainder of oil and sauté onion for approx. 3 minutes, add mushrooms and cook for a further 2 minutes. Add the wine and simmer for a further 5 minutes, add remaining ingredients. Pour sauce over the steaks and warm through before transferring to a serving dish. Garnish with a sprig of tarragon and serve with a green salad.

Comment: This is Dean's favourite pre–match meal to score goals on. The garlic keeps the opposition at bay!

ITALIAN SPAGHETTI SAUCE

Mrs Heather Travers, *Calgary, Canada*

Ingredients: **Serves 6–8**

½ cup onion slices
1 x 3 oz can mushrooms
2 x 8 oz cans tomato sauce
1 tsp chilli powder
1 bay leaf
¼ tsp thyme
2 large cans of tomatoes
2 tbsp oil
1½ lbs ground beef
¼ cup parsley
1 tsp salt
½ tsp pepper
1½ tsp oregano or sage
1 cup water

Method:

Brown beef and drain off the fat. Heat oil and cook onion; add beef and all other ingredients. Bring to the boil, lower heat and cook uncovered for approximately one hour. Divide into containers and freeze what is not needed.

Serving: Serve with spaghetti and tossed salad.

Comment: I have made this since we were first married and always have some in the freezer. When my daughter, Jessica, became a vegetarian, I left out the meat and substituted a tin of chickpeas which I put in the blender until they were completely smooth and then chucked them into the sauce.

VEAL MEDALLIONS WITH ASPARAGUS TIPS, LOBSTER AND HOLLANDAISE

Mrs Abi Clough, *Freelance Cook, Surrey*

Ingredients:

Serves 8

8 x 4–5 oz veal medallions
½ small cooked lobster
8 asparagus tips

Hollandaise:

2 egg yolks
4 oz butter
reduced vinegar, infused with bay leaf, onion, peppercorns

Method:

Seal veal medallions in hot butter and put into a roasting tin covered with foil. (This can be done a few hours before). Prepare the hollandaise — over a pan of cold water on a gentle heat; whisk the yolks and vinegar together in a bowl over the pan, until the water begins to simmer and when the mixture looks light and frothy. Continue whisking the mixture off the heat until the bowl is cool. Gently and slowly pour in the melted butter, continually whisking so as to prevent curdling.

Cook the asparagus for a few minutes until just tender in salted boiling water. Meanwhile cook the medallions for 10 minutes in a hot oven — 200C or until slightly pink inside.

Arrange the veal medallions on warmed plates, put the asparagus tips sliced in half lengthways on top together with pieces of lobster. Pour over a spoonful of hollandaise and decorate the plate with a sprig of watercress, bay leaves or fresh rosemary.

Comment: Fairly "last minute" but totally exquisite for that special something.

BUFFALO WINGS

Simon Hill, *Businessman — London*

Ingredients:

Serves 6

4 lbs chicken wings
4 tbsp butter
3–5 tbsp tabasco
celery sticks
1 tbsp white wine vinegar
2½ cups blue cheese dressing
salt and ground black pepper
oil for deep frying

Method:

Discard the wing tips and cut chicken wings into two pieces at the joint. Sprinkle with salt and pepper. Heat the olive oil in a wok or deep fat fryer to 375F. Add half of the wings and cook, stirring occasionally for about 10 minutes until crisp and golden. Remove with a slotted spoon and drain well. Repeat with remaining wings.

Melt the butter and add the vinegar and tabasco to taste. Pour over the chicken wings and serve with blue cheese dressing and celery sticks.

Comment: The main ingredient of Buffalo Wings is not, as you might first think, a buffalo. It is actually chicken but was invented in Buffalo, a city in New York State. Although Buffalo Wings can be easily produced at home the ideal environment to eat them is in a bar after a number of beers. They are the New Yorker's equivalent of having a curry after an evening in the pub and can be served in three ways — spicy, very spicy or just dynamite! It also helps that you don't have to leave the bar and find a restaurant.

Buffalo Wings are one of the most addictive of foods and are also great for parties. If in New York, call "Atomic Wings" on 86th Street and they will deliver a bucket of 50 for $24. Elsewhere, follow the recipe above!

CHICKEN IN AN APRICOT AND GINGER SAUCE

Anna Lee, *Principal of a nursery in Putney*

Ingredients:

Serves 4

4 chicken breasts
3 tsp soy sauce
2 tsp cornflour
1 oz butter
1 inch piece of fresh green ginger
15 oz can of apricots in syrup
1 spring onion

Method:

Roast chicken pieces for 15 minutes in a medium hot oven. Cover chicken with a few knobs of butter before cooking, so that it doesn't dry out. Peel the ginger and then cut into wafer thin slices (a potato peeler is good for this job). Then cut into shreds. Put apricots and their syrup into a pan and gently heat. Add ginger and soy sauce. Then blend in a blender until smooth and return to the pan. Bring gently to the boil and stir in cornflour. (Blend the cornflour with 2 tablespoons of water before adding). When the sauce has thickened add a sliced spring onion. Pour apricot and ginger sauce over chicken pieces and cook for a further 15 minutes in oven. Make sure that the dish is covered in the oven.

Serving: Serve with a green vegetable such as french beans or mange tout glazed with butter as this will add to presentation.

Comment: This recipe has a unique taste! The flavour of the chicken is enhanced by the contrasting sharpness of the ginger and the sweetness of the apricots.

CHICKEN BREASTS WITH CREAM CHEESE WRAPPED IN PARMA HAM

Mrs Liz Edkins, *Harpenden, Herts*

Ingredients: **Serves 4**

4 chicken breasts
4 slices of Parma Ham
4 oz cream cheese
Dijon mustard

Method:

Mix cream cheese and mustard to taste. Make a pocket in each chicken breast and put 1 oz of cream cheese and mustard mixture in it. Wrap each piece of chicken in parma ham and bake in baking dish covered with foil for 40 minutes at 190C. Take foil off after 30 minutes to give a nice golden brown and crispy finish.

Comment: A dish to impress!

CHICKEN WITH MINT AND AVOCADO

Suzi Hughes, *Party Organizer, London*

Ingredients:

Cooked chicken
Fresh mint
Equal quantities of soured cream and mayonnaise
Avocados
Mango chutney
Diced bacon for garnish
Salt, pepper & lemon juice

Method:

Mix soured cream and mayonnaise. Add mango chutney to taste and lots of chopped mint (the mint needs to soak in for a while to bring out the flavour). Add salt, pepper and lemon juice to taste. Stir in the cooked chicken pieces. Just before serving brush the avocados with lemon juice. Garnish with fresh mint, fanned avocado and diced bacon.

Comment: A refreshing alternative to Coronation Chicken!

CHICKEN & STILTON BOMBS

Mrs Francine Richardson, *Wife of Coventry City footballer Kevin*

Ingredients: **Serves 4**

4 large chicken breasts
2 oz butter
¾ bottle red wine
1 bunch watercress
4 oz stilton cheese
8 rashers streaky bacon
1 tbsp cornflour
seasoning

Method:

Blend Stilton and butter. Flatten out chicken breasts with a mallet, stuff and roll up breasts. Lay two rashers of bacon in a criss-cross and fold around each chicken breast, securing with cocktail sticks.

Place in a deep casserole dish and pour over wine, leave to marinate for a couple of hours. Cook at 170°C for 40 minutes or until golden brown. Remove onto a hot plate, drain off stock and place into a saucepan. Season, mix the cornflour with a little water whilst still stirring, bring to the boil.

Pour sauce over chicken breasts and garnish with watercress.

Comment: A really elegant dinner party dish with little or no effort.

EASY CHICKEN DIVAN

Mrs Elfie Fallowfield, *London*

Ingredients:

Serves 6–8

1 chicken or 3–4 chicken breasts
8 oz mayonnaise
½ cup mature processed cheese, grated
½ cup (approx) soft breadcrumbs
1 tbsp melted butter or margarine
2 tins condensed cream of chicken soup
1 tsp lemon juice
¾ tsp curry powder

Method:

Steam or simmer the chicken in stock until cooked. When cool, cut into pieces and slices and arrange in a greased baking dish (9½″ x 7½″ x 1½″). Place the breasts neatly on top and hide the small pieces below, when using the whole chicken!

Combine soup, mayonnaise, lemon juice and curry powder and pour mixture over the chicken. Sprinkle with cheese. Combine breadcrumbs and butter and sprinkle over the top. Bake at 350F or 180C for 25 to 30 minutes until thoroughly heated.

Serving: Serve with fresh or frozen broccoli spears, new potatoes and salad.

Comment: This dish is foolproof, delicious and deceptive! Prepare in advance and pop into the oven at the last minute. Adapt seasonings to taste.

LEMON CHICKEN

Mrs Jan Murray, *Churchill, Somerset*

Ingredients: **Serves 4**

6–8 pieces drumsticks
 or thighs of chicken
1 scant tsp tarragon leaves,
 freshly chopped
1 scant tsp basil leaves,
 freshly chopped
1½ oz butter
½ tsp thyme
2 tbsp lemon juice,
 freshly squeezed
salt and pepper

Method:

Place chicken pieces in an oven–proof dish. In a small saucepan, melt butter with lemon juice, herbs and seasoning. When you start to smell that heavenly aroma of the herbs and lemon, it is time to pour it over the chicken. Cook for 20–25 minutes at 400F, basting once if you have the time.

Comment: "Please may we have Lemon Chicken again?" This recipe is wheeled out regularly in our family with bright happy faces all round — the children's because they simply love it and mine because it is nutritious, quick and a doddle to do. Suitable for a dinner party or family supper.

MANGO AND MUSTARD CHICKEN

Jonathan Cumberlege, *Banker, London*

Ingredients: **Serves 6**

6 chicken breasts
1 tbsp of mango chutney
1 tbsp of Worcestershire sauce
1 tbsp of lemon juice
1 tbsp of apricot jam
½ cup of mayonnaise
2 tsp of grainy mustard

Method:

Put the chicken breasts in an oven-proof dish. Combine jam, chutney, mayonnaise, Worcestershire sauce, grainy mustard and lemon juice and pour over chicken. Cover dish with tin foil and leave to marinate for a few hours. Cook covered for 35 minutes at 180C.

Comment: My sister gave me this as the ultimate 'easy' dinner party dish. Can be prepared a couple of days in advance, only takes 5 minutes to prepare and tastes delicious — the perfect bachelor dinner party recipe!

ORIENTAL CHICKEN WITH NOODLES

Mrs Tish McVitie, *London*

Ingredients:

Serves 4

4 chicken breasts
2″ fresh turmeric root
1″ fresh galangal root
1 pkt egg noodles
3 tbsp or more olive/sesame seed oil
whole green beans
baby sweet corn
sliced french beans
small florets of broccoli and cauliflower
2 lime leaves*
2 stalks lemon grass, crushed
3–4 cloves garlic
1½ fresh ginger root
1 bunch fresh coriander
1 tin coconut milk
mange tout
baby carrots
soya sauce
fish sauce (salty)
sambal (hot chilli) sauce, small amount
ground black pepper
water

***Do not eat — remove before serving**

Method:

Grind coriander, turmeric, ginger, galangal and garlic cloves in food processor to make a paste. Skin and cut chicken breasts into strips. Prepare the vegetables, however much you want.

Heat oil in a wok and add herb paste. Add the sliced chicken and stir fry till cooked. Remove from heat and put into a dish. Add more oil to the wok if necessary, heat and add the vegetables in the order of longest cooking first, and stir fry for a few moments (ie par cook).

Add the cooked chicken, soya sauce, fish sauce (salty), sambal (hot chilli sauce — small amount) and ground black pepper. Add one whole tin of coconut milk and half a tin of water, stir and lay a packet of egg noodles (these come in three layers) on the top of this mixture. Cover and steam until the noodles are cooked. Stir them around and adjust the seasoning as necessary.

Comment: Serve in bowls with chopsticks. Delicious, filling and fun to do provided your guests are in the kitchen! You can get the fresh herbs from a good Chinese supermarket. Dried herbs are not the same.

RASPBERRY CHICKEN

Sarah Appleyard, *Party Organiser*

Ingredients:

Serves 8

8 chicken breasts
freshly ground pepper
and salt

1 pt double cream
⅓ pt raspberry vinegar

Poaching Mixture:

1 chicken stock cube
1 bay leaf
water

6 whole peppercorns
left over wine

Garnish:

1 small punnet of fresh raspberries
snipped chives

Method:

Place the chicken breasts in a shallow baking tray and cover with water, white wine, dissolved half stock cube, peppercorns and bay leaf. Cover in foil and cook in a pre-heated oven at 180C for between 15–20 minutes — do not over cook. You can leave the chicken wrapped in foil to keep warm. Meanwhile, reduce the raspberry vinegar i.e. simmer until it goes syrupy — about 5–7 minutes. Add a small amount (about 4 tbsp) of the poaching stock and re-boil for about 5 minutes. Add the other half of the crumbled stock cube. Add the double cream slowly and stir in with a pinch of salt and the freshly ground pepper, simmer gently for a few minutes.

Slice the breasts of chicken and arrange on a warmed plate. At the last moment gently add the fresh raspberries — do not stir. Pour sauce over the sliced chicken and sprinkle with chopped chives.

Serving: Serve with crisp green salad and hot new potatoes.

Comment: Fabulous for summer parties. Very easy but looks very pretty and also tastes delicious.

THAI CHICKEN CURRY

Mrs Caroline Hamilton, *Chef at Lodge Catering Ltd*

Ingredients: **Serves 4**

- 1 large clove garlic, crushed
- 1 tsp cumin seeds
- 1 or 2 red chillies, finely chopped
- 1 tsp Thai 7 spice seasoning
- 1 tsp ground coriander
- 1 dessertspoon medium curry paste
- 2 tsp oyster sauce
- 12 chicken thighs or 4 breasts skinned and chopped in large chunks
- 1 onion, sliced
- 1 tsp coriander seeds
- 1 x 2 inch piece fresh ginger
- 1tsp dried lemon grass
- 1 large can coconut milk
- ½ bunch fresh coriander
- 2–3 tsp sugar
- 4 oz ground almonds
- salt and pepper

Method:

Sweat onions, add cumin and coriander seeds until brown. Add garlic, chillis, ginger, ground coriander, Thai 7 spice and cook for a few minutes. Add chunks of chicken and brown all over. Add curry paste, coconut milk, oyster sauce, sugar and salt and pepper and simmer for 10 to 15 minutes. Thicken with the ground almonds. Before serving mix in fresh coriander, chopped.

Serving: Garnish with bunches of fresh coriander.

Comment: I made this up after being inspired by a 3 week trip to Thailand. It's really good with stir fried vegetables and egg noodles.

ROAST DUCK WITH CHERRY SAUCE

Tania Grossart, ***busy housewife expecting twins!***

Ingredients:

Serves 4

1 oven ready duck (4lb)
1 small onion, peeled and quartered
1 small cooking apple, quartered

Sauce:

½ pt chicken or vegetable stock
3 oz red cherries, pitted and roughly chopped
sliced fresh figs, cherries and parsley to garnish
1 tbsp clear honey
1 tbsp light soy sauce
1 fresh fig, wiped and roughly chopped

Method:

Pre-heat the oven 350F/180C/Gas Mark 4. Discard any fat from the inside of the duck, and then rinse and dry. Place the apple and onion in the cavity. Roast the duck on a trivet which allows it to stand proud of the roasting tin. Prick duck all over with a fork to allow fat to run out. Baste in its own juices several times. Bake for 25 minutes per pound and 20 minutes over.

Cherry Sauce: Heat together the chicken or vegetable stock, honey and soy sauce until honey has dissolved. Then boil rapidly and reduce by half. Add cherries and figs to pan and cook for 2 minutes. Pour into sauce boat. Serve with duck, garnished with watercress, cherries and sliced figs.

Comment: Great Christmas lunch alternative, or dinner party.

DUCK A L'ORANGE

Mrs Mary Cumberlege, *Braunton, Devon*

Ingredients:

Serves 4

1 duckling (4–5 lbs)
2 tbsp dry red wine
2 level tbsp redcurrant jelly
2 oranges, juice and
  coarsely grated rind
1 level tbsp flour
½ wine glass sherry
  seasoning to taste

Garnish:

2 oranges, thinly sliced
  watercress

Method:

Wash duckling inside and out with cold running water. Dry with kitchen paper. Prick skin all over with a fork. Sprinkle well with salt, then stand the bird on a grid in a roasting tin. Put in centre of moderate oven, 180C/350F/Gas Mark 4, and cook — allowing 25 minutes per lb. DO NOT baste or cover. Transfer to warm platter and keep hot. Pour off all but 1 tbsp fat from roasting tin. Stand tin over medium heat and stir in flour. Cook for 2 minutes without browning, add orange rind, juice, wine, jelly and sherry. Cook gently, stirring, until jelly dissolves and sauce comes to boil and thickens. Season to taste, and simmer for 2 minutes.

Serving: Pour some sauce over the duck and serve the rest separately. Garnish duck with a border of orange slices, and bunches of watercress.

Comment: A really delicious duck recipe that is incredibly quick and easy. Allow plenty of meat per person.

PHEASANT POT-ROAST

Patrick Reger, *Director of Appeals — SSAFA*

Ingredients: **Serves 6–8**

3 pheasants
5 oz butter
1 tin Campbell's condensed consommé
1 generous glass brandy or calvados
salt and black pepper
8 oz thin streaky bacon
5 oz double cream
a few mushrooms
garnish with watercress
cornflour

Method:

Season birds, truss feet and cover with bacon. Butter base of cast-iron cooking pot, put birds in and dot with remaining butter. Cover with tight-fitting lid, sealed with foil and cook in oven at 220C/425F/Gas Mark 7. After 45 minutes, remove pot from oven and add flaming brandy/calvados. Pour in cream and consommé to cover birds half way up, return to oven with pot lid off. Cook for 15-20 minutes or until birds are tender and bacon and breasts are brown. (If not ready, pour large drink and try to take your guests' minds off things until birds are done!)

Remove birds to dish and hack into manageable portions. Thicken juice in pot with a tablespoon of cornflour — add brandy if necessary. Pour some of this sauce over birds and return dish to oven to keep warm.

Serving: Serve birds garnished with a good strong green vegetable (I prefer calabrese), mashed potatoes, redcurrant jelly and perhaps ratatouille on a side dish. Any juice remaining next day makes marvellous soup.

Comment: "Far too good to give to people you don't like!"

PHEASANT SALAD

Mrs Shirley Ann Cumberlege, *Ross-Shire, Scotland*

Ingredients: **Serves 4**

1 pheasant
2 sticks of celery
2 or 3 hard boiled eggs
red or white wine vinegar
butter for roasting
few cooked new potatoes (sliced)
1 raddichio lettuce
1 frisée lettuce
olive oil
Hellmann's mayonnaise
horseradish
salt and pepper

Method:

Roast the pheasant in butter. Leave slightly underdone. Prepare a salad of raddichio and frisée lettuce, a couple of sticks of celery and some cooked new potatoes. Dress the sliced potatoes lightly with a dressing made of olive oil, a little Hellmann's mayonnaise and some wine vinegar. Season.

Make a bed of the salad. When the pheasant is cooked remove from roasting tin and cut into pieces (joint). To the cooking juices add some red wine, horseradish, salt and pepper and a little olive oil. Simmer for a minute. Put the pheasant pieces back in this juice to coat them. Place the pheasant and the juices artistically on the salad and surround with the hard boiled eggs cut longways into 4. It should be served neither hot nor cold but tepid.

Comment: What to do when the family are sick of roast pheasant .

ROAST PHEASANT WITH WHISKY AND RAISINS

Mrs Annie Charlesworth, *PA/Conference Organiser, Wiltshire*

Ingredients: **Serves 4**

1 pheasant
2 oz butter
watercress (garnish)
6 rashers rindless bacon
2 slices crustless bread

(Stuffing):

2 oz raisins
2 tbsp whisky
13 oz Philadelphia cream cheese
gravy made from giblets etc.

Method:

Stuffing should be prepared in advance and the gravy can be prepared at the same time. Mix whisky, cream cheese and raisins together and leave to stand for 24 hours. Stuff pheasant with raisin mixture and cover breast and legs with the butter and bacon rashers.

Toast bread and cut each slice in two and sit the pheasant on these in a roasting pan. Pre–heat oven to 400F/Gas Mark 6 and roast pheasant on centre shelf for about 50 mins, basting from time to time. Remove bacon and cook for a further 10 minutes to brown pheasant breast. Take out of oven and place pheasant on a carving dish surrounded by toast and watercress.

The easiest timing is to put bird in oven 1 hour before guests are due to sit down to dinner. While the first course is being eaten, cover the bird with foil and keep it hot in a low oven. This will allow additional cooking time, if necessary, of 10–15 minutes.

Comment: A different way of cooking a pheasant and a great favourite with my husband!

FILLET OF LAMB CASSEROLE

Molly Beer, *Colchester, Essex*

Ingredients: **Serves 6**

2 lbs fillet of lamb
1 aubergine
1 large onion
6 tomatoes, skinned
mixed fresh herbs, chopped
salt and pepper
4 courgettes
8 oz mushrooms
2 cloves of garlic
1 rounded tbsp brown sugar
1 tsp mace

Method:

Cut up lamb — chunks or sliced and fry in butter, add onion, garlic, sliced courgettes, cubed aubergine and brown. Add sugar and herbs and put in a casserole in its own juices for 30 minutes — 150C oven. Add chopped tomatoes, mushrooms and cook for another 30 minutes.

Comment: Very, very tasty!

STUFFED LOIN OF LAMB

Lady Wilsey, *Bulford, Wiltshire*

Ingredients: **Serves 6**

2 lbs loin or best end of neck
2–3 tbsp dripping

Stuffing:

2 tbsp chopped onion
5 tbsp fresh breadcrumbs
1 orange, grated rind
2 tbsp chopped mixed herbs (fresh)
1 oz butter
beaten egg
seasoning

Sauce:

1 onion
redcurrant jelly
½ pt stock
orange juice

Method:

Bone lamb or ask the butcher to do this! Make the stuffing, cook onion in butter until soft, add to crumbs, herbs, orange juice, rind and seasoning, bind with beaten egg. Spread over inside of meat and roll up and tie securely. Roll in seasoned flour, egg and browned crumbs. Roast for one hour at 370F. Make gravy adding finely chopped onion, redcurrant jelly and stock, boil up well, season and add orange juice.

Comment: Rather fattening because you keep wanting more!

LAMB WITH APRICOTS

Toby Tennent, *Shropshire*

Ingredients:

Serves 4

2 oz dried apricots
4 oz dried black eye beans
1¼ lb boned casserole lamb
2 level tbsp flour
½ level tsp chilli seasoning
1 level tbsp ground coriander
salt and milled pepper
1 tbsp oil
4 oz onions, skinned & sliced
4 oz mushrooms, wiped & sliced
1 pt light stock
3 level tbsp mango chutney
5 oz carton natural yoghurt
snipped parsley

Method:

Soak apricots and beans separately overnight. Boil the beans for 10 minutes in salted water; drain.

Marinate the lamb overnight (12 hours) in olive oil, wine, curry powder, coriander, any spice you find in the cupboard, etc. When the time comes to brown the lamb use part of the marinade as the frying oil, this makes a thick flavoursome goo, which adds to the taste.

Cut the lamb into 1 inch cubes. Toss it in the flour seasoned with chilli, coriander, salt and pepper; brown, a few pieces at a time, in the hot oil in a flame proof casserole dish. Remove from the fat, using a draining spoon. Add the onion and mushrooms and fry for a few minutes. Stir in the stock, beans, chutney, and dried apricots. Replace the lamb. Bring to the boil, cover and cook at 170C/325F/Gas Mark 3 for about 1 hour, until the meat is quite tender. Stir in the yoghurt, adjust the seasoning. Garnish with parsley.

To Freeze: Cool, pack and freeze. To use, thaw overnight at cool room temperature, reheat gently on top of the stove.

STIR FRY LIVER

Mrs Di Freeman, *Yorkshire*

Ingredients:

Serves 4

1 lb liver, lamb or pigs, cut into thin strips
1 inch piece of fresh root ginger peeled and finely chopped or grated
watercress to garnish (opt)
seasoned flour
2 tbsp oil
1 oz butter
1 small onion, thinly sliced
6 oz button mushrooms, sliced
2 tbsp redcurrant jelly
4 fl oz chicken stock

Method:

Toss liver in seasoned flour. Heat the oil and butter in a large frying pan or wok and stir–fry the liver, onion, ginger and mushrooms for 3–4 minutes. Add redcurrant jelly to stock, pour into pan and heat through stirring and tossing until the jelly has melted. Serve immediately.

Comment: This is quick, easy, economical and delicious — serve with tagliatelle or rice and salad or a green vegetable.

TRANCHE of CALF'S LIVER, SAUCE BERCY

Marco Pierre White, *Chef Extraordinaire*

Ingredients:

Serves 4

6 oz thin slices calf's liver
salt and freshly ground white pepper
plain flour
vegetable oil

Garnishes:

2 lb baby spinach leaves, washed thoroughly
8 wafer thin slices streaky bacon
Sauce Bercy
2 oz unsalted butter
2 fl oz water
4 large fresh sage leaves

Sauce Bercy:

10 shallots, finely sliced into rings
17 fl oz red wine
¼ oz unsalted butter
salt and freshly ground white pepper
5 fl oz port
10 fl oz veal stock
1 tsp double cream

Method: (Sauce)

Marinate the shallots in the port for 24 hours and cook in the port until soft. Cool in the port, then strain, keeping both. Reduce the port and red wine together by four-fifths, down to about 4½ fl oz.

Add the veal stock to this reduction and bring to the boil. Boil to reduce to a good sauce consistency. Add the cooked shallots and whisk in the butter along with the cream. Taste and correct seasoning.

Method: (Tranche of Calf's Liver)

Cook the spinach in the water and butter for a few minutes only until just wilted. Season with salt and pepper, then drain. Keep warm.

Grill the bacon until crisp. Deep-fry the sage leaves in hot vegetable oil for a few seconds until crisp. Drain well.

Season the raw liver slices with salt and pepper, and flour lightly. Heat 2 fl oz of the vegetable oil in a large wide pan and fry the liver until golden brown on each side and pink in the middle, about 3–4 minutes in total.

Place the spinach in the middle of the warm plate, and arrange the liver on top. Place the crisp bacon on top of the liver along with the sage leaves. Serve with pomme purée to garnish.

LAMB AND CHEESY PASTA CASSEROLE

Mrs Jo Blythe, *housewife and mother*

Ingredients: Serves 6–8

6 oz tagliatelle
1 lb minced lamb
8 oz full fat soft cheese
6 spring onions (chopped finely)
1 tbsp of finely chopped
 green pepper
1 tbsp sunflower oil
14 oz tin of tomatoes
8 oz cottage cheese
3 tbsp natural yoghurt
4 tbsp water
salt and pepper

Method:

Cook tagliatelle as directed on packet and drain. Heat oil in pan and fry the lamb until brown. Stir in the tomatoes, water and seasoning and remove from heat. Combine remaining ingredients in a separate bowl. Spread half the tagliatelle in a 4 pint casserole dish. Cover with half the cheese mixture and the mince and repeat. Preheat oven to Gas Mark 5/190C/375F and bake uncovered for 30 minutes.

Comment: This light pasta and lamb casserole is a delicious contrast between the rich lamb and tangy soft cheeses. Quick and easy to make and always goes down a treat — clean plates all round! If you haven't got time just cook the pasta and the lamb and tomatoes and mix the cheese mixture into the hot pasta and serve without casseroling.

MY PASTA (PASTA CASA NOSTA)

Susannah York, *Actress*

Ingredients:

Serves 5 or 6

2 or 3 cloves of garlic
2 or 3 bay leaves
1 green & red pepper
black olives, to taste
oregano, to taste
dash of tomato paste
large packet fresh pasta
or thin spaghetti
1 onion (optional) (spring onions are even better)
1 lb tomatoes, or 2 tins of tomatoes — or mixture
½ lb mushrooms (optional)
fried aubergine, delicious!
salt & pepper
olive oil

Method:

Into a pan of boiling salt water, to which you've added a teaspoon of olive oil, drop the pasta. About 5 minutes does it. Meanwhile add chopped garlic and onions to some olive oil in a pan. Add chopped tomatoes, herbs, and all, or some of the other ingredients. If you have half a glass of wine handy, add that too. Serve separately with plenty of freshly grated parmesan.

Comment: Carnivores and vegetarians respond very favourably! But not good for picnics.

PASTA WITH ROSEMARY AND CHILLI

Alistair Little's *Cookery Weeks in Italy*

Ingredients: **Serves 3–4**

2 cloves of garlic, finely chopped
2 small dried red chilli peppers
1 sprig of rosemary
salt and pepper
12 sage leaves
2 bay leaves
4 tbsp olive oil
14 oz spaghetti

Method:

Soak the chilli peppers for a few minutes in water and chop finely. Put a large pan of lightly salted water on to boil. Put oil, garlic, chilli and herbs in a frying pan and heat over a gentle flame until infused — do not burn the garlic. Meanwhile cook the pasta for 8–9 minutes, when al dente drain and return to the hot pan. Pour the warm seasoned oil with its herbs onto the spaghetti and toss thoroughly. Season to taste, mix again and serve immediately.

Comment:

It is generally a good idea to reserve about half a pint of the pasta cooking liquid a few seconds before you drain — this can be added in small amounts when tossing the spaghetti if it appears to be dry and is also particularly useful in this recipe because it emulsifies the oil and makes it more digestable.

PASTICCIO DI RIGATONI E POLLO

Mrs Christabel Cumberlege, *Norton sub Hamdon, Somerset*

Ingredients: **Serves 7–8**

1 x 4 lb chicken or 3 lb chicken joints
14 oz rigatoni or penne pasta
3 oz fresh parmesan, grated or good cheddar
¼ pt white wine or dry vermouth
fresh herbs or dried oregano
1 stick of celery, chopped
scant handful of breadcrumbs
salt and pepper
18 oz broccoli
4 oz butter
1 onion, quartered
1 carrot, quartered
4 tbsp flour
¼ pt double cream
parsley stalks

Method:

Put onion, carrot, celery and herbs into a large casserole. Add jointed chicken and barely cover with water, season. Bring to boil gently, then simmer for ½ hour.

Take out chicken pieces, remove the meat from the bone and cut into sizeable pieces. Replace bones in stock and simmer for a further 1½ hours. Strain.

Cook broccoli in boiling salted water until barely tender — drain and divide larger chunks into bite sized portions. Heat 3 oz butter in a saucepan, add flour and cook very lightly, stirring for 2 minutes.

Pour on all the wine or vermouth and bubble fiercely. Stir in 1¼ pints of the chicken stock, whisk sauce briskly for a few minutes. Fold in ¾ of the cheese. Season and when cooler, add the cream.

Cook the pasta "al dente", drain and toss with remaining butter. Put layer of pasta first into large (preferably wide and shallow) ovenproof dish, add ⅓ chicken, ⅓ broccoli, ⅓ sauce and sprinkling of remaining cheese. Continue filling dish in layers. Top by sprinkling breadcrumbs on top and the rest of the cheese and dot with more butter.

Bake in a pre-heated oven, 425F/220C or Gas Mark 7 for 25 minutes. (I make this up to final baking stage the previous day, and make sure ingredients are quite cool before combining).

Serving: Delicious with a green salad.

Comment: Oven pasta dish — takes a while to prepare — luckily in advance — tastes divine!

PRAWN & PASTA SALAD

Darcey Bussell, *Principal Dancer, The Royal Ballet*

Ingredients:

Pasta shells — cooked
hard boiled eggs
herb salad
mushrooms
French mustard
mangetouts — blanched & refreshed
½ lb (approx.) prawns
iceberg lettuce
cherry tomatoes
extra virgin oil
lemon juice
ground pepper

Method:

Mix all fresh ingredients together and season with ground pepper and dressing (extra virgin oil, freshly squeezed lemon juice and French mustard).

Comment: As I am not into cooking, I can put together a cold pasta and prawn salad quite easily.

SPICY PASTA

Sting and Trudie Styler, *Wiltshire*

Ingredients: **Serves 3–4**

- 4 sun–dried tomatoes (soaked and chopped)
- 1 chopped red chilli pepper (depending on taste)
- 4 shiitake mushrooms, soaked and chopped
- ½ pt passata (sieved tomatoes)
- 2 cloves of garlic
- 4 fresh tomatoes
- olive oil
- small bunch of chopped basil
- cooked spaghetti

Method:

Heat olive oil and add all the ingredients, with the exception of the garlic and passata. Cook to a thick paste, then add the passata and garlic. Leave to cook for at least five minutes. Mix with cooked spaghetti.

Comment: When having to entertain unwanted guests, treble the chilli!!

BACON RISOTTO

The Rt Hon Mr John Major, *Prime Minister*

Ingredients: **Serves 4**

2 oz butter
4 oz sliced mushrooms
6 oz cooked bacon/ham
7 oz can sweetcorn with peppers
1–1½ pts stock
(or water and a stock cube)
1 large onion, chopped
6 oz long grain rice
4 oz cooked peas
pepper
sultanas (optional)

Method:

Melt butter in large frying pan, add chopped onion and cook gently for 5 minutes. Add mushrooms, stir round and cook for a few seconds. Stir in rice and one pint of stock. Cover and cook gently for 20–25 minutes until rice is cooked. If necessary add extra stock. Cube bacon and add to the rice with the remaining ingredients and season with pepper. Cook for a further 5 minutes to heat through; taste and add salt if required. If liked, a few sultanas may be added.

Comment: All in one meal which is tasty but easy and quick to prepare. For a full and satisfying meal serve with a salad and crusty French bread or rolls.

CHINESE PORK FILLET

Mrs Barbara Fegen, *Thames Ditton, Surrey*

Ingredients:

Serves 4

1½ lbs pork tenderloin
4 cloves garlic, crushed
1 tsp 5 spice powder
2 tbsp sesame seeds
2 tsp finely grated fresh root ginger
2 tbsp hoisin sauce
3 tbsp honey
4 tbsp soy sauce
1 cup hot water
6 tbsp cold water

Method:

Put tenderloin into a roasting pan and mix all ingredients together, except hot water, and rub this marinade well over the meat. Stand aside for at least 1 hour or, preferably, leave overnight in fridge. Heat oven to Gas 5 and cook meat in the tin slightly above centre for approximately 55 minutes, basting after ½ hour and again 15 minutes later. When pork is cooked, lift out of tin and slice, and put on a warm serving dish. Add hot water to marinade and juices in tin and bubble for a few minutes. Spoon some of this over the meat and serve rest separately.

Comment: Delicious, different, and well received by all my guests who always ask for the recipe!

HAM ROLLS FROM THE PIDDLE VALLEY

Mrs Gay Hanbury, *Secretary-Housewife*

Ingredients: **Serves 4**

8 slices of well shaped ham
4 leeks (1–1½″ diameter)

Cheese Sauce:

1 tbsp butter
8 small sliced mushrooms (opt)
milk and vegetable water
salt and pepper
flour to thicken
grated/diced Leicester cheese to taste (2–6 oz)

Method:

Cut leeks in half and cook in boiling salted water for about 7 minutes until firm but not soggy. Drain leeks, keeping some water for the sauce.

Roll one piece of ham round each half leek and arrange on top of the rice. Put into a moderate oven (or on top of pan of boiling water) while you make a thick cheese sauce which you then pour over the ham rolls. These are transferred either to a hot oven or under a grill until starting to brown (3–4 minutes).

Sprinkle with parsley and serve immediately with a side salad. You can substitute leeks with 4 sticks of cooked celery, or asparagus.

Serving: Serve on a bed of rice (2 oz per person) and decorate with chopped parsley.

Comment: Attractive and infinitely adaptable; tart up for dinner parties or make–do on 2 camping gas rings! (This is the recipe that my son, Richard, wanted to learn when he came out of Salisbury District Hospital because it's so easy and looks professional!)

PORK ESCALOPES WITH GINGER AND CREAM

Mrs Ruth Williams

Ingredients: **Serves 6**

6 escalopes of pork
2 tbsp lemon juice
3 pieces preserved ginger
  drained of syrup and chopped
2 tbsp flour, seasoned with
  salt and pepper
2 oz butter
¼ pt soured cream
2 fl oz water
1 tbsp oil
¼ pt green ginger
  wine

Method:

Coat each fillet in seasoned flour and shake off excess. Heat the butter and oil in frying pan. Sauté escalopes until they are browned on each side and cooked through, about 6 minutes. Remove them from the pan and keep them warm on a serving dish in a low oven. Pour into the frying pan the ginger wine, lemon juice and water, and stir well. Let it boil away until the liquid has reduced by half, then stir in the sour cream and chopped ginger. Boil again until the sauce has thickened, then pour it over the cooked escalopes and serve with rice or new potatoes and a green vegetable.

Comment: This can be prepared in minutes but looks and tastes wonderful; the sauce is very rich and gingery.

PORK AND PRUNES

Miss E A Mullin, *Bishop's Stortford, Herts*

Ingredients: **Serves 4**

1½ lb pork fillet or shoulder
½ lb prunes
½ pt stock
2 tbsp flour
1 tbsp wine
  butter

Method:

Flour and season pork. Fry in butter until brown, then place in casserole dish. Add stock to pan and simmer and then strain over pork. Add wine and prunes and cook in oven at 180C for about one hour, or until tender.

Comment: Quick, easy and very tasty.

VEAL OR PORK MAINTENON

Mrs Di Freeman, *Minskip, York*

Ingredients: **Serves 4**

4 escalopes (veal or pork)
1 shallot, finely chopped
1 tsp tomato purée
1 glass of sherry
1½ oz butter
2½ fl oz stock
1 tsp flour
salt and pepper

Salpicon:

4 mushrooms, sliced
1 oz butter
1 tbsp sherry
2–3 oz ham, cooked and shredded
1 shallot, finely chopped
½ oz flour, scant
a little good stock

Mornay Sauce:

1 oz butter
½ pt milk
1 oz flour
2 oz grated cheese

Method:

Sauté escalopes in butter until golden brown on both sides, allowing about 10 minutes in all. Remove escalopes from the pan, press flat and keep warm. Add chopped shallot to pan and cook until golden. Stir in flour and allow to colour, then blend in tomato purée, sherry and stock. Bring to the boil, season and simmer for 2-3 minutes. Strain and keep hot.

(Salpicon): Sauté mushrooms and shallot in half the butter. Season, add flour and a little stock. Bring to the boil again and add the sherry and ham.

(Mornay Sauce): Melt the butter, add the flour and cook for a couple of minutes. Gradually add the milk, simmer and add the cheese, until a nice coating consistency.

Put the escalopes in an oven proof dish and cover each with the salpicon. Coat with mornay sauce, dust with a little extra cheese and dot with remaining butter. Brown in a hot oven or under grill. Pour round hot gravy. If entertaining, this can be prepared in advance and then baked in oven at 375F/Gas Mark 5 until hot and browned.

Comment: Inspite of the different stages it's easy, quite rich and always enjoyed. It freezes well too!

VEGETARIAN

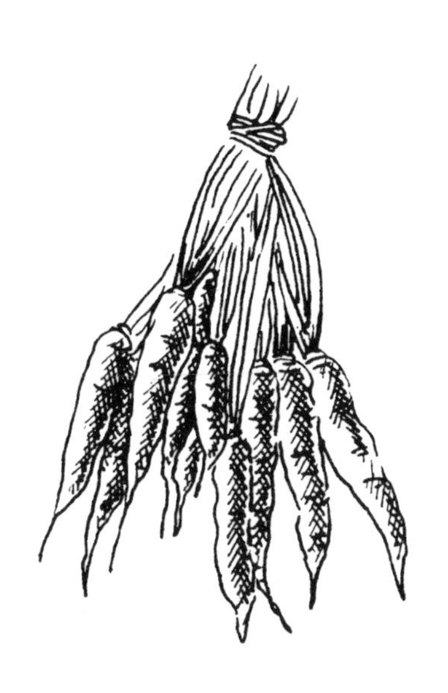

AUBERGINE, TOMATO & RED PEPPER TERRINE

Annie Fryer, *Annie Fryer Catering Ltd*

Ingredients: **Serves 6–8**

2 large aubergines
4 fl oz olive oil — preferably virgin
½ lb ripe tomatoes, preferably plum
2 cloves garlic, crushed
⅛–¼ pt jellied chicken stock
4 red peppers
2–3 tbsp pesto OR
4 tsp ground cumin
basil, chopped

Method:

Slice aubergines lengthwise, sauté in oil, drain. Trim to long rectangles to fit the terrine, reserve trimmings. Cut peppers in half lengthwise, remove seeds, drizzle with olive oil, roast in a hot oven until soft, trim to long rectangles, reserve trimmings. Peel, slice and deseed tomatoes. Magimix the aubergines and pepper trimmings with the basil, garlic and pesto/ cumin. Season.

Line terrine with tin foil, and brush with oil. Layer peppers evenly to fit the base add thin layer of purée, add aubergine followed by purée. Place tomato slices in even layer. Warm the stock and pour over a little to moisten. Bake reg. 375F/190C/Gas Mark 5 for 10-15 minutes until firm. Chill. Turn out and serve decorated with basil leaves.

Comment: Serve on its own with salad and garlic bread or with cooked chicken, turkey etc.

CARONATA

Mrs Rokie Shiffner, *Bath*

Ingredients:

Serves 6–8

¾ lb large aubergine
¾ lb courgettes, chopped into cubes
¼ lb mushrooms, chopped
¼ cup red wine vinegar
4½ oz tin pitted black olives, drained
1 tin tomatoes (16 oz)
1 cup celery, chopped
½ cup salad oil
1 cup onion, chopped
½ tsp oregano
½ tsp garlic powder
1½ tbsp sugar
½ tsp dried basil
1½ tsp salt

Method:

At least 3½ hours before required cook aubergine and courgettes in 12″ skillet on medium heat for 15 minutes. Stir occasionally till tender but still crisp. Stir in all remaining ingredients except olives (tomatoes plus liquid) — simmer gently 20 minutes, till fork tender. Spoon into large bowl, add olives, check seasoning, cover and refrigerate till well chilled. Keeps well.

Comment: On a lunch stop–over with a friend in the USA I enjoyed this vegetable dish so much that I was given the recipe. It has never failed, though it's better if one remembers to add all the ingredients — it's especially easy to forget the olives!

GRILLED MEDITERRANEAN VEGETABLES

Miss Prue Leith, *cookery writer and broadcaster*

Ingredients: **Serves 6–8**

2 small aubergines
6 spring onions
2 heads of fennel
extra virgin olive oil
2 courgettes
6 medium field mushrooms
1 large red pepper
1 large yellow pepper

(For Garnish):

fresh basil leaves
squashy black olives
sea salt
extra virgin olive oil
coarse freshly ground black pepper

Method:

Heat grill, grill pan, barbecue or oven broiler to maximum. Slice the fennel into thick slices, leaving some stalk–end on each slice to hold the leaves together. Use a swivel peeler to remove the thin outer membrane of the peppers. Then cut them into sections down the creases and peel any edges previously missed and cut each section in half.

Slice aubergines and courgettes in ¼″ thick (lengthwise) strips, trim and slice the spring onions in half (lengthwise if thick) and remove tough stems from the mushrooms. In a large bowl, turn all the vegetables in olive oil to coat.

Arrange vegetables on the grill, grill pan or on a foil-covered grill tray. Grill at the maximum heat to char both sides. Remove as they are done.

Serve warm or cold, drizzled with additional olive oil, seasoned generously with sea salt and freshly ground black pepper. Garnish with sprigs of fresh basil and a few black olives.

VARIATIONS:

(Brushetta)

Serve warm on thick slices of country bread fried in olive oil, or brushed with olive oil and grilled.

(Dinner party starter)

Arrange attractively on individual plates and shave parmesan cheese on top, using a vegetable peeler.

Comment: This dish is the only way to make something as boring as a courgette taste wonderful and it has the advantage of being good hot, great lukewarm, delicious cold and irresistible the next day.

ITALIAN BAKED ASPARAGUS

Penny McIntosh, *Bedale, North Yorkshire*

Ingredients: **Serves 4**

1 lb uncooked asparagus spears
2 tbsp onion, finely chopped
2 tbsp celery, finely chopped
1 tbsp freshly grated parmesan
pinch of thyme
2–4 tbsp butter
1 tbsp breadcrumbs
1 tin chopped tomatoes
pinch of oregano
salt and pepper

Method:

Melt butter in bottom of rectangular baking dish. Line bottom with asparagus spears. Sprinkle with the onion, celery, cheese, breadcrumbs and chopped tomatoes (drained). Season with salt, pepper, oregano and thyme. Cover and bake in preheated oven (180C, 375F, Gas Mark 4) for about one hour.

Comment: Very useful as a change when you have a glut of asparagus. It's good.

LITTLE MUSHROOM PIES

Nicola Cox, *Cookery Writer*

Ingredients: **Serves 6**

(Mushroom Filling):

½–¾ lb mushrooms
1 oz butter
1 tbsp plain flour
1 tbsp parsley, finely chopped
1 clove garlic, finely chopped
a little chopped fresh or
pinch dried lemon thyme or thyme
dash of tabasco sauce OR
cayenne pepper
2–3 shallots OR
1 onion, finely chopped
4–5 tbsp yoghurt, sour
cream or cream
freshly grated nutmeg
squeezed lemon juice
egg wash
salt and pepper

(Cream Cheese Pastry):

3 oz soft butter
6 oz plain flour
3 oz cream cheese
good pinch of salt

Method:

(Pastry) Cream the soft butter well, beat in cream cheese, sift in flour and salt and work to a dough. Knead briefly into a flat disc and rest in a plastic bag in the fridge for about ½–2 hours.

(Filling) Melt the butter in a frying pan and fry shallots or onion until softened. Slice and add mushrooms, cutting the slices in halves or quarters if they are large, add chopped garlic and fry over high heat until lightly cooked, moisture has evaporated and butter is again apparent (sometimes mushrooms in autumn can be very watery and you have to remove them from the pan and boil the liquid away before returning them and continuing). Sprinkle over flour and cook for a moment or two; then add yoghurt, spoonful by spoonful, stirring all the time and letting it cook into the dish so that it does not curdle. Season with tabasco or cayenne, nutmeg, seasoning and chopped herbs, add a good squeeze of lemon juice and cook until thick and creamy. Cool the mixture.

Roll pastry thinly and cut bottoms and lids to fit mince–pie tins. Lay in the bases and fill with a teaspoon of the mushroom filling. Moisten lids around the edge with cold water and press in place. Prick the tops, brush with egg–wash and bake in a hot oven (400F/200C/Gas Mark 6) for 15–20 minutes until crisp and brown. Serve hot or cold.

Comment: These yummy little pies are from Nicola's book. They are made with cream cheese pastry and a spiced mushroom filling for a nice first course, picnic or savoury. You can keep the uncooked pies or the prepared filling in the freezer.

MARINATED MUSHROOMS

Mrs Ann Hughes, *Colchester, Essex*

Ingredients:

Serves 4

4 fl oz wine vinegar
1 small onion, finely chopped
1 lb button mushrooms or sliced mushrooms
2 tbsp tomato purée
fresh coriander to garnish
½ clove garlic
1 bay leaf
3 tbsp oil
seasoning

Method:

Put the vinegar, garlic, bay leaf and onion into a saucepan. Bring to the boil and simmer until the onion is tender. Add the tomato purée and oil. Mix together thoroughly and season to taste. Pour the marinade over the mushrooms, cover and leave overnight in the refrigerator. Remove the garlic and bay leaf. Garnish with coriander.

Comment: Delicious and useful recipe — and it can be made the day before!

MUSHROOM ROAST

Sue Cook, *Television Presenter*

Ingredients:

Serves 4

1 large onion, peeled and chopped
½ pepper, red or green (deseeded and diced)
1 tbsp chopped parsley
8 oz cheese, grated
2 tbsp oil
12 oz flat mushrooms
4 oz brown breadcrumbs
3 eggs, beaten
salt & pepper to taste

Method:

Heat oil in frying pan, add onion and cook for 5 or 6 minutes until transparent. Add diced pepper and continue cooking for 2 minutes, stirring occasionally. Add mushrooms and cook for a further 2 minutes. Stir in breadcrumbs, beaten eggs, half of the grated cheese, salt and pepper. Spoon mixture into an 8 inch greased cake tin and sprinkle the remainder of the grated cheese on top. Bake for 30 to 40 minutes at 425F/220C/Gas Mark 7. Turn out of the tin and cut into slices before serving, sprinkled with parsley.

POTATO CAKES

Dame Judi Dench, *Actress*

Take any left-over mashed potatoes and put into a good-sized bowl. Sieve plain flour into the potatoes, mixing as you go, until you have a stiff dough. Add salt and pepper to taste.

Roll out on a well floured board to 1½ inch thickness. Cut into squares or other shapes, you can make diamonds or triangles or circles if you like, and put on a dry hot griddle. You can also cook them in a heavy frying pan. Cook until they are brown on both sides, then split and butter.

Serving: They are delicious served with bacon.

Comment: An extremely delicious way of using up left-over potatoes!

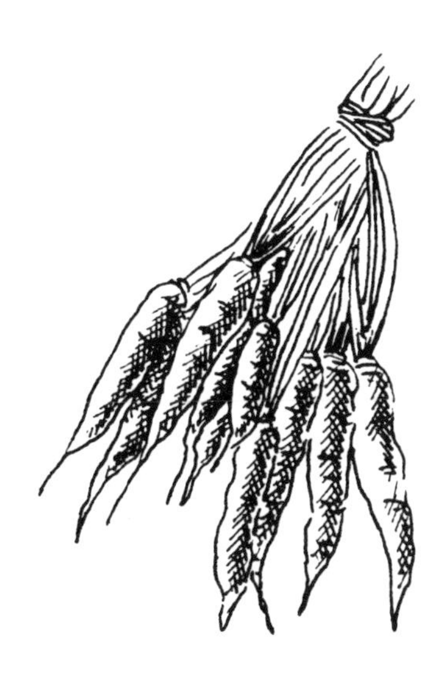

POTATO GRATIN – Provençal Version

Binda Large, *Fressingfield, Suffolk*

Ingredients: **Serves 6**

3 lbs potatoes
1 onion
4 oz strong cheese, grated
(parmesan is best)
1 glass red or white wine
1 pt well–flavoured stock
2 + tbsp olive oil
salt and pepper
garlic (unlimited!)

Method:

Peel, rinse and slice potatoes thinly. Slice onion, finely. Peel garlic, chop or slice. Heat stock and add wine. Pour 2 tbsp olive oil into bottom of a shallow gratin dish. Put in a layer of potato, then a layer of sliced onion and garlic. Add half the grated cheese and rest of the potatoes. Season as you go. Pour in the hot stock. Trickle some more olive oil over surface, and cover dish with foil. Cook gently in the oven for 50–60 minutes, depending on depth of baking dish. Keep dish covered for first half hour, then uncover and sprinkle on rest of the cheese. Allow to finish cooking and gild a rich brown.

Comment: This dish goes down well with anyone who enjoys lots of garlic and olive oil. Can be served with just a green salad, or goes well with good sturdy meat dishes such as proper French sausages.

SAVOURY NUT ROAST

Lord Attenborough, *Actor/Film Director*

Ingredients: **Serves 4**

2 oz walnuts, minced or liquidised
2 oz cashew nuts, minced or liquidised
4 oz brazil nuts, minced or liquidised
4 oz tomatoes, skinned and sliced or quarter pint tinned tomatoes, drained
2 tbsp wheatgerm or 1 level tbsp onion soup mix, if preferred
1 small onion
1 oz butter or oil
1 tsp (level) mixed herbs or thyme
2 eggs
salt and pepper

Method:

Fry onion in the butter or oil — add to other ingredients and mix thoroughly. Pack into greased fireproof dish or tin. Brush top with melted butter or oil. Bake on top shelf of oven at 350F/Gas Mark 4 for 40 minutes until brown. Serve hot with gravy or onion sauce, greens and potatoes or cold, sliced with salad, chips or rolls and butter.

Comment: Very easy to make and is excellent hot or cold.

SCALLOPED POTATOES

Jack Gardner, *Executive Director, INSPIRE*

Ingredients:

Serves 4–6

8 potatoes, sliced
1 onion, sliced
1 tin cream of mushroom,
  celery or chicken soup
4 oz breadcrumbs
2 oz butter
  salt and pepper to taste

Method:

Slice potatoes and onions in rounds and layer alternatively in a casserole dish; season with salt and pepper. Pour on soup and sprinkle the bread-crumbs on top. Dot with pieces of butter. Preheat oven and bake at 325F/170C/Gas Mark 3 for 1¼ hours.

Comment: Good enough to eat.

THIS & THAT

CHEESE ON TOAST

Coventry City Football Club PLC
Coventry

Dear Vanessa

Thank you for your recent letter. My favourite meal is, in fact, cheese on toast — it's certainly the only thing I can cook!

I wish you every success with your project.

Yours sincerely

Ron Atkinson
Manager

CHOCOLATE SAUCE

Mrs Jo Cumberlege, *East Woodlands, Somerset*

Ingredients: **Serves 4**

1 oz chocolate powder
1 tbsp butter
¼ cup boiling water
1 cup of caster sugar
¾ tsp vanilla essence
(put in last)

Method:

Boil all the ingredients up together and simmer for 5–10 minutes.

Comment: Nothing better to go on vanilla ice cream — it's always a huge hit! Goes hard and toffee-like as soon as it's put on the ice cream, not very good for one's fillings!

CRAB SAVOURY

Mrs J Young, *St Albans*

Ingredients: **Serves 4**

½ lb crabmeat
1 pkt Philadelphia cream cheese
3 tbsp finely chopped spring onions
⅓ cup of lemon juice
¼ cup mayonnaise
⅛ tbsp garlic salt

Method:

Marinate crab in lemon juice for about 1 hour. Blend remaining ingredients. Drain crabmeat and add to ingredients. Serve well chilled on Jacob's cream crackers, crispbreads or crispy rolls.

Comment: Makes a perfect Bridge snack.

FUDGE

Jeremy Bird, *Aldershot, Hampshire*

Ingredients:

2 lb sugar
1 tin sweetened condensed milk
essence to flavour
4 oz butter
½ cup milk

Method:

Swish cold water around a large saucepan, just enough to wet it. Put all the ingredients (except essence) in the pan and melt slowly. Bring to the boil stirring all the time. Boil for 15–20 minutes, still stirring and then remove from the heat and beat the mixture until it thickens. Best done in the open air as it gets rid of the steam quickly. Beat in the flavouring — a few drops of vanilla or almond essence — and pour into a flat dish to set.

For a really outrageous treat cover the hardened fudge with a thin layer of chocolate and dust with icing sugar. (I prefer it without the chocolate or icing, they really are too much for me).

Comment: My mother had the recipe memorised, as all the family were treated to their own special tub every birthday and Christmas. It will be a particular favourite for all those people out there that have an exceptionally sweet tooth. My father adores it!

MEAT LOAF

Dr & Mrs F P Willis, *Westow, York*

Ingredients: **Serves 6**

1 lb cold meat (mixture of lamb, beef or chicken)
1 pkt of sage and onion stuffing
stock or gravy
salt and pepper
½ lb liver
6 oz bacon
1 medium onion
bayleaves

Method:

Chop up the onion, meat, liver and bacon in a food processor. Add the stuffing and moisten with the stock or gravy. Grease an oven-proof dish or mould. Place slices of bacon and bayleaves in the bottom and fill with the mixture. Bake in a moderate oven standing in a dish of water. Turn out when cold.

Comment: This is a quick, cheap dish that will freeze well and is unlikely to poison the family!

PEAR CHUTNEY

Marchioness of Bath, *Longleat*

Ingredients:

3½ lb pears
1½ lb sugar
1 lb seedless raisins
½ pt vinegar
1 tsp powdered allspice
1 tsp powdered cinnamon
1 tsp powdered cloves
2 oranges

Method:

Peel, core and chop the pears. Grate the rind of the oranges and squeeze out the juice. Add rind, juice and pears to the spices, raisins, sugar and vinegar, and bring to the boil. Reduce heat and simmer for 1½ hours. Pour into warm jars and cover tightly.

Comment: From the 17th century merchants brought home to England a variety of pickles which quickly became popular.

SOME KIND OF SALAD

Michael Kreiger, *Playwright* — *New York City*

Ingredients: **Serves 4**

½ lb mixed salad leaves
¼ lb Prosciutto ham
2 lemons
2 dollops of honey
¼ lb Parma ham
1 blood orange
splash of Scotch whisky
olive oil

Method:

Squeeze the lemons into a mixing bowl and add olive oil until it looks okay (I think it was quite a bit). Add the honey, mix it up and add the whisky. Peel the orange and cut orange into cubes (make sure you don't get any pith). Add it to the dressing. Arrange the greens and ham on a serving plate (I put the ham around the outside). Pour the dressing on top.

Comment: (I bought the salad leaves already mixed, I believe they were weeds rather than lettuce as I noticed dandelion leaves. There were also some very attractive edible flowers in there). I hate salad. I have always hated salad. I can't tell you how many salads I have sat through while wishing it were a bacon sandwich. Salad is awkward to eat. It is unsatisfying. It is boring. Like rice, as a matter of fact, and that is something I also hate. In America we are taught that anything except rice and salad will cause you to become fat and die as a miserable and round-shaped recluse. The above salad is my answer to the salad freaks. This is a cease-fire in the war on flab.

Patient: Doctor... If I quit smoking, eat right, stop having sex will I live longer?

Doctor: No, but it might seem longer!

STEM GINGER TRUFFLES

Cynny Sharp, *Stockbridge, Hampshire*

Ingredients:

8 oz plain chocolate, melted
2 tbsp stem ginger, chopped
3 tbsp stem ginger syrup
1 oz butter
3 tbsp whipped double cream

Method:

Mix all the ingredients together. Chill in fridge until stiff enough to roll into balls. Coat in cocoa/vermicelli and wolf down!

Comment: Yummy! Useful for presents, fetes or dinner parties!

STILTON AND SESAME BISCUITS

Chris Suter, *Head Chef*
Bishopstrow House Hotel, Warminster, Wilts

Ingredients:

4 oz plain flour
4 oz stilton
4 oz butter
2 oz sesame seeds

Method:

Beat butter and stilton until almost smooth. Add flour and bind until you have a dough. Chill slightly, then roll into balls the size of a large marble. Now roll the balls through the sesame seeds till totally encrusted. Refrigerate. Place balls onto a greased tray. Flatten slightly, then bake till golden brown on 160C–170C for 7 minutes.

Comment: Easy to make, a real tasty teasing nibble before dinner to get everyone licking their lips and dying for the next course!

THUNDER AND LIGHTNING

Miss Katie James, *Battersea, London*

Three steps to a slice of heaven:

Make some French toast (for best results, slices of baguette soaked in beaten egg and milk, then lightly fried in butter till golden). Generously drizzle Golden Syrup on top.

Then dollop with Cornish clotted cream (for maximum enjoyment!) or extra thick whipped double cream.

Alternatively, if you are lazy, substitute French toast for brown sliced bread rolled round the Golden Syrup and cream and enjoy!

Comment: This idea came to Ness and I whilst suffering an appalling attack of cabin fever–munchies and equally bad hangovers on a rainy, summer's afternoon stuck inside a mobile home caravan with 12 friends in Polzeath, Cornwall!

TINNED DELIGHT

Sam Vallings, *Model*

Ingredients:

1 tin peeled tomatoes
1 tin baked beans
1 tin frankfurters
1 bottle chilli sauce

Method:

Add ingredients to saucepan and heat till hot. Add chilli sauce to taste. Serve immediately with fresh bread, covered with lashings of butter.

Comment: Fast, filling and not that horrid. Sounds like a good bachelor recipe Sam — but not one to impress the girls!

WONDERFUL ORANGE SAUCE

Mrs Cynny Sharp, *Wiltshire*

Ingredients:

4 oz sugar
½ pt water
1 tbsp marmalade
2 cloves
arrowroot to thicken
1 orange
½ beef stock cube
1 tsp cornflour
sprig thyme
vinegar

Method:

Boil sugar and orange juice to a copper colour. Add dash of vinegar and water and boil. Add cloves, thyme, beef cube, strips of orange rind and marmalade. Simmer and thicken with arrowroot.

Comment: This will keep up to 2 weeks in a fridge. Delicious with sausages, duck, ham, etc.

NOTES

PUDDINGS

ABBOTTS BARTON (Raspberries)

Emma Madden, *Freelance Cook, Surrey*

Ingredients: **Serves 4**

1 lb frozen/fresh raspberries
½ pt natural yoghurt
½ pt double cream
soft brown sugar

Method:

Place the raspberries on the bottom of a glass bowl or if you prefer in individual dishes. Lightly whip the cream until it stands in soft peaks. Fold in the yoghurt and place on top of the raspberries. Sprinkle a very generous amount of soft brown sugar over the top. Cover with clingfilm and leave in the fridge for 24 hours. The sugar then caramelises and soaks into the yoghurt mixture.

Comment: A very easy and very yummy pudding.

APPLE TART with a Calvados Sabayon

Simmy Hooper,
Owns a catering company called "Selbys", in London

Ingredients: **Serves 6–8**

(Pastry)

6 oz butter
5 oz caster sugar
½ tsp vanilla
1 dessertspoon lemon juice
8½ oz flour
2½ oz ground almonds
1 egg

(Filling)

4 oz nibbed almonds
3 oz unsalted butter
cinnamon
6 dessert apples
5 oz sugar
½ tsp vanilla

Method:

(Pastry) Put the flour in a magimix and add the butter in small pieces. Pulse until like breadcrumbs. Add ground almonds and sugar and pulse. Add egg, lemon and vanilla mix until it forms a ball. Be careful NOT to over mix. Chill pastry. Line the flan dish and chill again.

(Filling) Peel, quarter and slice apples. Cream butter and sugar and add vanilla, cinnamon and almonds. Layer apples in the uncooked pastry case. Dot the almond mixture over the apples. Bake at 400F/200C/Gas Mark 6 for 40 minutes — until golden. The apples go caramelly and the pastry goes shiny.

(Calvados Sabayon)

Ingredients:

1 tbsp of caster sugar
6 tbsp of dry white wine
2 egg yolks
1 tbsp of Calvados

Method:

Mix ingredients together and then whisk over hot water until thick (about 5 minutes). It can sit for about 10 minutes before collapsing, therefore serve immediately, next to the apple tart.

Comment: The best apple tart recipe I have ever tried — the almonds form a praline making it caramelly and delicious. Very easy to make and no need to pre-cook the pastry first. Freezes very well.

BANOFFI PIE

Mrs Belinda Evans, *Kensington, London*

Ingredients: **Serves 8–10**

4 oz butter
3 bananas
½ pt whipped cream
20 digestive biscuits
1 tin of condensed milk
toasted flaked almonds

Method:

Crush the biscuits and put in a dish and cover with the melted butter (put in fridge). Boil the condensed milk for 2 hours in its tin and make sure it is constantly covered with water. Cool, open carefully and pour onto biscuit base.

When cold, cut bananas, cover toffee with them and put whipped cream immediately on top (to stop the bananas going brown). Decorate with toasted flaked almonds.

Comment: Sumptuous and very easy!

BOOZY BANANAS

Barney Morison, *Director of Pineneedle Ltd Publishers — London*

Ingredients: **Serves 6**

6 bananas
1 cup of dark rum
4 oz flaked almonds
1 cup of fresh orange juice
2 oz brown sugar
½ pt double cream

Method:

Cut bananas in half lengthways. Place in an open oven–proof dish and add the orange juice and rum. Sprinkle the brown sugar over the top and bake in the oven for half an hour at 180F. Grill the almonds until they are lightly browned, then sprinkle them over the bananas and serve with cream.

Comment: Probably the most delicious pudding in the world!

CARAMEL PEACHES A LA PIKE

Mrs Hew Pike, *Sandhurst, Surrey*

Ingredients: **Serves 6**

6 ripe peaches
6 oz dark brown fine sugar
6 oz unsalted butter
3 tbsp double cream

Method:

Blanch, skin, halve and de-stone six ripe peaches. Put them into individual dishes, or slice and put into one larger serving dish.

Sauce: Put the butter and sugar into a heavy based saucepan and gently heat until the butter has melted and the sugar has dissolved. Boil until the mixture glistens like toffee (not too long or it will become too hard and set when cold). Add the double cream and mix in well. Leave to go cold, stirring occasionally to ensure a smooth, shiny texture. Pour the sauce over the peaches shortly before serving.

Comment: This is quite delicious and decadent.

CHERRY SOUP

Chris Suter, *Head Chef*
Bishopstrow House Hotel, Warminster, Wilts

Ingredients: **Serves 6**

1 bottle Côte du Rhone (red wine)
8 oz sugar
2 tsp cornflour
2 lbs fresh cherries
24 mint leaves
1 tsp water

Method:

Wash and stone the cherries. Mix the sugar and wine in a thick bottomed pan. Bring to the boil then simmer for a couple of minutes. Mix cornflour and water then whisk into the simmering wine. Whisk or stir until slightly thickened then strain into a clean pan. Add the cherries and cook for 3 to 4 minutes. Remove from the heat and immediately insert the mint leaves. Allow to infuse for 2 hours then refrigerate. Serve well chilled with a good vanilla, cinnamon or Kirsch ice cream.

Comment: A beautiful cold summer treat perfect for meals al fresco or serve as an accompaniment to a lemon cheesecake.

CHOCY MERINGUE PUDDING

Mrs Jo Cumberlege, *East Woodlands, Somerset*

Ingredients: **Serves 6**

(Meringue)
6 egg whites
14 oz caster sugar
2 tsp vinegar
2 tsp vanilla essence
2 tsp (level) cornflour

(Filling)
3 oz caster sugar
3 tbsp of water
3 egg yolks
6 oz unsalted butter
2 oz plain chocolate
1 oz cocoa

Method:

(Meringues) Whisk egg whites until VERY stiff but not dry. Mix cornflour, vinegar and vanilla essence and whisk in with the sugar. Spread 2 or 3 rounds of meringue mixture on bakewell paper and put in a preheated oven 150°C — then turned down to 140° — for 1 hour. Turn oven off and leave meringue cases in until cold.

(Filling) Dissolve sugar and water in a heavy based pan, simmer until syrup makes a thread (about 5–10 minutes). Beat yolks in bowl and pour syrup over, stir till mixture cools and then stir in the butter in little pieces. (If it curdles add a tablespoon of melted butter and stir vigorously). Melt chocolate in a bowl over hot water — add cocoa and a little water until you have a smooth porridge mixture. Add this to the butter cream. Spread in layers between meringues. Cover with cream and toasted flaked almonds a couple of hours before serving. THIS IS BETTER IF MADE 2 DAYS BEFOREHAND.

Comment: This is a marvellous dinner party recipe as the meringue and chocolate mixture can both be made a few days in advance. For any special occasion at home, the family always ask for this pudding.

CHOCOLATE MOUSSE ALLA ROMANA

Jill Cucco, *Rome, Italy*

Ingredients: **Serves 4**

2 eggs, separated
5¼ oz Mascarpone cream cheese
3½ oz bitter chocolate
(opt.) Amaretti biscuits
2 tbsp sugar
2 tbsp liquid coffee flavouring

Method:

Beat egg yolks and sugar together with a wooden spoon till fluffy and light. Add cheese gradually, beating in well with a wire whisk until a smooth cream. Melt chocolate and coffee over very hot water, then add flavouring (e.g. rum, cognac, vanilla). Cool. Stir well into cream mixture. Whip egg whites and fold in. Pour into glass dish or individual glasses.

Optional:

Put crumbled Amaretti biscuits in the bottom of the glass. Decorate the mousse with a blob of whipped cream (not necessary, but it looks good and adds a few more calories).

Comment: No good at all for Weight–Watchers!

CREME BRULÉE, POMMES SEC, JUS de GRANNY SMITH

Gordon Ramsey, *Head Chef at The Aubergine*

Ingredients: **Serves 10**

1¼ pts double cream
4 vanilla pods, split
16 egg yolks
10 Granny Smith apples
8 fl oz milk
4¾ oz caster sugar
brown demerara sugar

Garnish:

3 Granny Smith apples

Method:

Mix cream, milk, sugar and egg yolks together in a bowl. Scrape vanilla seeds into the liquid and add the pods as well. Leave for an hour or so for the vanilla to flavour the liquid, then remove the pods.

Pour the mixture into individual small 3″ ramekins, place in a bain–marie, and cook in the oven preheated to 100C/212F or a very low gas, for 1½ hours.

Remove from the oven, leave to cool in the bain-marie, then refrigerate. Turn the creme brulées out of their moulds an hour before serving.

Peel, core and very, very thinly slice three of the apples (use a mandoline, so that the slices are virtually transparent). Place on a baking sheet and dry in the oven preheated to 150C/300F/Gas 3 for about 45 minutes until they become crisp.

Cut each of the remaining 10 apples into four pieces, skin, core and liquidise. Remove the froth.

Place the brulées on a tray or on individual plates. Powder the demerara sugar in a strong processor and sprinkle over the tops of the brulées. Using a blow torch, or a preheated grill, caramelise the tops. Clean the plates of any excess sugar.

Pierce all round the sides of the brulées with slices of dried apple, so that each one looks like a fan. Pour the apple 'juice' around the outside of the brulées.

Comment: This well–tested recipe looks more complicated than it is — recipe can be halved.

PLOP PUDDING

Capt Chris Kuhle, *Army Officer*

Ingredients:

Serves 4

1 cup of flour
2 tbsp cocoa
2 oz melted butter
1 cup of sugar
½ tsp baking powder
1¼ cups boiling water

Method:

Mix the flour, ½ cup of sugar, 1 tablespoon of cocoa and the baking powder together, and add the 2 oz of melted butter and sufficient milk to make it into a "dropping" consistency. Put into a dish and pour over the sugar, water and cocoa powder. Do not mix.

Put dish into a tin of water and into the oven for 30–40 minutes. This needs experimentation to get a hard crust on top and a "gooey" consistency with lots of chocolate sauce underneath.

Comment: I haven't the faintest idea what heat (quite hot) but ideal is the top oven in an Aga. If you love "Death By Chocolate", you'll love this even more!

RHUBARB FUDGE CRUMBLE

Nigel Laughton, *Helicopter Pilot*

Ingredients:

Serves 4–6

1½ lb rhubarb (cut into pieces)
1 orange, grated rind & juice
3 oz sugar (white or brown)

For the Fudge Crumble:

1 tsp (rounded) ground cinnamon
6 oz digestive biscuits, crushed
4 oz demerara sugar
4 oz butter

Method:

Mix rhubarb, orange rind, juice and sugar and put into an oven proof dish. Cover the dish with a piece of foil and bake, for approx. half an hour, until rhubarb is soft but firm 350F, 180C, Gas Mark 4. Cool. Melt butter in saucepan, stir in the demerara sugar, digestive crumbs and cinnamon. Cook for 5 minutes, stirring occasionally. Cover the cooked rhubarb with the fudge topping and bake for 15–20 minutes 400F/200C/Gas Mark 6.

Comment: In theory this should be enough for 6, however, it is normally devoured prior to serving. Serve hot with ice cream or cold with whipped cream.

ROAST FIGS

Sebastion Snow, *Chef at Snows on the Green*

Ingredients: **Serves 8**

4 tbsp and 1 tsp caster sugar
2 oz shelled walnuts, chopped
3 turns of pepper mill
crystallized lemon rind

1 oz unsalted butter
18 figs
1 lemon (juice)
2 tbsp honey

Method:

Preheat oven to 180°C/350°F. Butter a shallow baking tray; place figs in it side by side, stems up. Sprinkle with 4 tbps of sugar and 1 tbsp water. Bake for 15 minutes, basting figs every few minutes. Add chopped walnuts and sprinkle with the remaining sugar. Lower oven temperature to 130C/280F and bake for 5 minutes more. Transfer figs and walnuts to serving dish; add honey to cooking juices; set on top of stove and stir over a low heat to blend. Spoon over figs; sprinkle with lemon juice and pepper. Top with crystallized lemon rind.

Comment: Excellent summer dish to finish off any meal. Roasting brings the sweetness out of the figs which, together with lime or lemon, leaves a very clean refreshing flavour on the palate.

SCRUMPTIOUS WHITE CHOCOLATE CHEESECAKE (uncooked)

Charles Cumberlege, *Frome, Somerset*

Ingredients: Serves 6–8

7½ oz white chocolate
11 oz soft cream cheese
5 oz sugar
½ large pkt of digestive biscuits
¼ pt double cream
3 egg whites
1 egg yolk
2 oz butter

Method:

Melt the chocolate and wait until it is semi–cold. Fold it into the cream cheese which has been mixed with the double cream. Whisk egg whites and sugar together and fold into mixture. For added richness and staying power you can add an egg yolk. To make the base, blend the crushed biscuits with the butter (melted) and line an 8 inch flan dish. Pour the mixture on top and put the cake in the fridge for about an hour until it sets.

Comment: A big favourite with everyone.

SEATTLE, USA CHEESE CAKE

Mrs Sally McMillan, *Bristol, Avon*

Ingredients:

Serves 6

(Filling)
1 lb Philadelphia cream cheese
2 tsp vanilla
4 oz cream
2 eggs, beaten
½ lemon, juice and rind
4 oz sugar

(Pie Crust)
Digestive biscuits
Butter

(Topping)
8 oz sour cream
1 tbsp sugar
1 tsp vanilla

Method:

Line 10″ glass pie dish with mixed crushed biscuits and butter and bake 5 minutes at 450F. Blend well the filling ingredients and put into pie crust, sprinkling the lemon rind on top. Bake 20 minutes at 350F. Mix sour cream, sugar and vanilla and spoon in blobs onto cake and bake for another 5 minutes. Sprinkle finely ground digestive biscuits on top and serve very cold. Best made day before.

Comment: This is an excellent cheesecake recipe — easy to make too!

ZEBRA CAKE

The Baroness Cumberlege CBE DL, *Lewes, Sussex*

Ingredients: **Serves 6**

1 pkt ginger biscuits
½ pt double cream, whipped semi-stiff
dry sherry

Method:

Take biscuits one at a time and dip one side into a saucer of sherry and spread one side of the biscuit with whipped cream. Place on side onto oval dish. Take the next biscuit and after dipping in sherry and spreading with cream sandwich next to previous biscuit. Continue until all the biscuits are used forming a roll on the plate. Cover the roll with remaining cream. Leave for 12 hours in the fridge. Cut diagonally when serving in slices. Decorate with crumbled flakes.

Comment: Ideal for dinner parties.

ICE CREAMS

AFTER EIGHT ICE CREAM

Gill Lewis, *Tilford, Surrey*

Ingredients: **Serves 4**

1 oz sugar
6 oz After Eight mints
¼ pt double cream
¼ pt water
3 egg yolks

Method:

Dissolve sugar in water and bring to boil over moderate heat, boil for 3 minutes. Put mints in blender and add syrup. Blend thoroughly and add egg yolks. Cool a little and then quickly blend in the cream. Put in large bowl or small ramekins and freeze. Best served straight from freezer.

Comment: Delicious pudding and takes 5 minutes to make!

BLACKBERRY ICE CREAM

Mrs Vivian Charlesworth, *Salisbury, Wilts*

Ingredients: **Serves 4**

1 lb blackberries
4 oz icing sugar
1 tsp lemon juice
½ pt double cream

Method:

Blend the blackberries in the liquidiser and then put the puree through a sieve to extract the seeds. Stir in the icing sugar and lemon juice. Whip cream until thick and fold in the blackberry puree. Freeze. When mixture gets icy, turn sides into centre and stir well to ensure a creamy smooth consistency.

Serving: Take out of freezer and put into fridge 30 minutes before serving. Decorate with a few blackberries.

Comment: I make this a lot when blackberries are in season. It has a lovely delicate flavour.

CRUNCHIE BAR ICE CREAM

Mrs Annie Andrews, *Warminster, Wiltshire*

Ingredients: **Serves 4**

1 tin sweetened condensed milk
2 Crunchie bars
½ pint double cream

Method:

Whip cream until it reaches the soft peak stage. Add condensed milk and stir in chopped up Crunchie bars. Freeze until firm.

Serving: Best served with mixed summer fruits or berries.

Comment: Pure heaven!

LEMON AND ORANGE ICE CREAM

Mrs Penny Roblin, *Bere Regis, Devon*

Ingredients: **Serves 4**

6 egg yolks
2 small oranges, grated rind and juice
1 lemon, grated rind and juice
8 oz caster sugar
½ pt double cream

Method:

Whisk egg yolks and sugar until thick and creamy. Gradually whisk in rind and juice of oranges and lemon. Whisk double cream and fold into egg mixture. Turn into a carton and freeze.

Comment: Very refreshing and perfect for a summer party.

RHUBARB AND GINGER SORBET

Mrs Cynny Sharp, *Stockbridge, Hampshire*

Ingredients: **Serves 4**

6 oz sugar
1 lb rhubarb
2 tbsp syrup from ginger
¼ pint water
1 piece of stem ginger
1 egg white

Method:

Dissolve sugar in water over low heat. Boil, add rhubarb and cook gently until tender. Stir in finely chopped ginger and syrup and purée the mixture. When cold freeze until mushy. Whisk egg whites until stiff, fold through mushy mixture and freeze again. Leave in fridge to soften a little before serving.

Comment: This is very refreshing and inexpensive. Serve it with shortbread or really good ginger biscuits.

STRAWBERRY ICE CREAM

Lady Williams, *Strete, Devon*

Ingredients: **Serves 4**

1 pint sweetened fruit purée
½ pt lightly whipped cream

Method:

Take 1 pint of sweetened fruit purée and freeze. When required thaw and beat well adding ½ pint of lightly whipped cream and freeze again for approximately 12 hours. Take out of freezer approximately 1 hour before serving and put in refrigerator.

Comment: Strawberries, which normally do not freeze well, are excellent for this. Other soft fruits, i.e. black and redcurrants are also good. Sweetened purée may be kept in freezer for the winter!

TEA TIME

BANANA CAKE

Louise Bruce, *Preston, Lancashire*

Ingredients:

2 oz butter or margarine
2 large eggs
8 oz self raising flour
pinch of salt
5 oz caster sugar
2 ripe bananas
pinch of salt

Method:

Preheat oven to 375F/190C/Gas Mark 5. Put all the above ingredients into a food processor until mixed. Then put into a well greased 1½lb loaf tin. Bake for 1 hour in the middle of the oven until loaf is golden brown and coming away from the sides.

Comment: Brilliant for using up over ripe bananas and delicious while still warm with lots of butter. Takes just minutes to make.

BOILED FRUIT CAKE

Lady Redwood, *Corton, Wilts.*

Ingredients:

1 lb mixed dried fruit
8 oz margarine or butter
1 cup cold water (7 fl oz)
1 level tsp bicarbonate of soda
1 level tsp baking powder
6 oz brown sugar
10 oz flour
2 eggs

Method:

Bring dried fruit, brown sugar, butter, water and bicarb to the boil. Remove from heat and cool slightly. Add the eggs, flour and baking powder. Mix well and pour into 8″ cake tin. Bake for 1–1½ hours at Gas Mark 5.

Comment: This recipe was in the Staff College Cook Book from the 1970 course. It became a family favourite then and has remained so ever since. Very easy to make and very easy to eat!

CARROT CAKE

Jacky Pope, *London*

Ingredients:

8 oz self–raising flour
5 oz granulated sugar
6 oz vegetable oil
7 oz carrots (grated in Magimix)
2 oz walnuts (chopped)
2 oz sultanas

1½ tsp baking powder
1¼ tsp baking soda
½ tsp cinnamon
½ tsp salt
3 eggs (beaten)

Topping:

5 oz cream cheese
2 oz melted butter
4 oz sifted icing sugar

1 tsp vanilla essence
3 tsp lemon juice

Method:

Sieve flour, baking powder, baking soda, cinnamon and salt. Beat eggs till thick, slowly adding oil. Fold in dry ingredients and carrots alternatively. Fold in nuts and fruit. Pour mixture into 2 greased and floured 8″ deep sandwich tins and bake for 35 minutes, then cool. Topping: beat cheese until smooth. Slowly mix together with butter. Fold in icing sugar and beat in vanilla and lemon. Chill for 1 hour. Spread between cakes and on top.

Comment: For carrot cake lovers — one of the best!

CHOCOLATE AND ORANGE CAKE

Granny Cumberlege

Ingredients:

2 oz caster sugar
2 oz butter or margarine
2 level tsp golden syrup
1 orange, finely grated rind
6 oz crumbled sweet biscuits
(eg digestives or rich tea)
2 oz chocolate powder

Orange Water Icing:

Icing sugar
water
1 orange squeezed and rind
finely grated

Method:

Cream together margarine, sugar and syrup until very soft. Add orange rind, chocolate powder and crumbled biscuits. Work well together with a wooden spoon until quite smooth. Press into a sandwich tin which has been lightly oiled. Leave for an hour or so to set. Cover cake with a thin layer of orange water icing.

Comment: A grandchild's dream!

CHOCOLATE CAKE

John Hopping, *Norton sub Hamdon, Somerset*

Ingredients:

9 oz plain chocolate
4 oz caster sugar
4 eggs, separated
6 oz butter
7 oz ground almonds
5 tbsp apricot preserve

Method:

Preheat oven to 180C/350F/Gas Mark 4. Line base of a 8½″ spring form cake tin and brush with melted butter. Melt 6 oz chocolate over boiling water. Cream 4 oz butter with the sugar until light and fluffy, stir in almonds, egg yolks and melted chocolate, beat together.

Whisk egg whites until stiff and fold into mixture, pour into tin and bake for 50–55 minutes until firm to touch. Leave for a few minutes then turn out onto a wire rack and leave to cool.

Coat top of cake with the apricot conserve. Cut the remaining butter into small pieces and put with chocolate and melt, stir and spread over top of cake and let it dribble down the sides. The cake may sink slightly when cooling, but any cracks in the surface will be covered by the chocolate topping.

Comment: John Hopping trained as a chef in Paris and this cake was the highlight of the "teas" at the local Somerset History Exhibition.

CRUNCH

David Juxon, *Helicopter Pilot*

Ingredients:

3 oz butter
1 dessertspoon of golden syrup
6 oz porridge oats
4 oz caster sugar

Method:

Melt butter, sugar and syrup then add the oats. Press into a shallow tin. Bake at 300F/150C/Gas Mark 2 for 12 minutes.

Comment: A little more golden syrup added and they're even more sticky and more–ish.

DATE AND WALNUT LOAF

Mr and Mrs Barry Lewis, *London*

Ingredients:

12 oz plain flour
2–3 tbsp milk
½ pt apple purée
¾ teaspoon bicarbonate of soda
6 oz butter or margarine
1 tsp cinnamon
6 oz chopped walnuts
6 oz chopped dates

Method:

Rub butter and flour to breadcrumb consistency. Add sugar, cinnamon, dates and nuts. Make a well and stir in apple purée and finally mix the bicarbonate of soda with the milk and add to the mixture. The dough will be quite stiff — stir just enough to mix.

Put in lined loaf tin and cook (375F/190C/Gas 5) for about 1¼–1½ hours. (In a fan oven it seems to take just over an hour).

Comment: Excellent either spread with jam or on its own and freezes well. No eggs are needed — heaven knows how it hangs together!

DOUBLE CHOCOLATE CHIP BROWNIES

Mrs Jenny Toyne Sewell, *London*

Ingredients:

Makes 16 2″ brownies

2 oz unsweetened chocolate
5 oz sugar
½ tsp baking powder
1 tsp vanilla essence
2 eggs, slightly beaten
2½ oz unsalted butter
2½ oz plain flour
2½ oz chopped pecans
5 oz chocolate chips

Method:

Preheat oven to 350F. Melt the butter and chocolate and combine with the sugar, flour, baking powder and vanilla. Stir well. Add the eggs when cool and stir in the chocolate chips. Cook for about 30–40 minutes. It is very important that it is not over-cooked or the brownies won't be moist and gooey in the middle.

To make them even more delicious I sometimes make a **CHOCOLATE GANACHE** to go on top of them:

½ pint double cream
½ lb chocolate

Bring the cream to boiling point, take off heat and immediately beat in the chocolate — this will melt and make the most scrummy, rich, shiny icing. It sets when cool.

Comment: As a big fan of anything chocolatey this is the nicest brownie mixture I have discovered yet and delicious as a pudding with vanilla ice cream and chocolate sauce — naughty but nice!

FAT GIRLS FUDGE CAKE

Liney Abbott, *Codford, Wilts*

Ingredients:

1 lb 2 oz digestive biscuits
3 oz soft brown sugar
1 lb mixed dates, glacé cherries, chopped cashew and hazel nuts
2 tbsp golden syrup
6 oz butter/margarine
½ pt milk

Method:

Break up digestive biscuits into small pieces. Mix with the chopped fruit and nuts. Bring golden syrup, sugar, butter and milk to the boil, and cook until mixture begins to thicken. Add to the biscuit mix, place in an 8″ container and press. Cool and allow to set.

Comment: This delicious biscuit cake is not for the figure conscious!

KEMPTON COOKIES

Lady Vallings, *Long Ditton, Surrey*

Ingredients:

4 oz butter
1 tbsp boiling water
1 cup self-raising flour
3 oz sugar
1 tbsp golden syrup
1 cup porridge oats

Method:

Mix everything together and roll into 1 inch balls. Place on silicone baking paper and put in oven at 400F for about 20 minutes.

Comment: Very popular in the traffic jam when trying to leave the race course!

NUTTY GOOEY TOPPING CAKE

Zannie Abbott, *Student at Norwich University*

Ingredients:

(Sponge)
4 oz sugar
4 oz butter
4 oz self raising flour
1 level tsp baking powder
2 level tsp ginger
½ tsp salt
2 eggs

(Topping)
1 oz soft brown sugar
1 oz flaked almonds
1 oz chopped cherries
1 oz sultanas
2 oz butter
1 tbsp golden syrup

Method:

Grease and line a loaf tin. Melt topping ingredients and pour into tin. Mix all dry ingredients together and rub in the butter to resemble breadcrumbs. Add eggs and mix together for 2 mins — pour on top of topping mixture. Bake Gas 4/350F for 45–50 mins. Turn out.

Comment: Exceedingly good cake despite being really sticky!

MILLIONAIRES' SHORTBREAD

Mrs Carol Pratt, *Yorkshire*

Ingredients:

Base:

5 oz plain flour
2 oz sugar
4 oz butter
pinch of salt

Filling:

4 oz butter
4 oz soft brown sugar
1 small tin condensed milk
2 tbsp golden syrup
drop vanilla essence

Topping:

melted chocolate

Method:

For base, rub ingredients together and press in tin and bake at 325F then leave to cool in tin.

For filling, put butter, sugar, syrup and milk into pan — stir over gentle heat until sugar has dissolved. Bring to boil and stir for 7 minutes. Add vanilla and beat well. Cover shortbread base and leave to cool. Cover with melted chocolate.

Comment: Delicious, but not very slimming!

ORANGE BUTTER SPONGE

Mrs Biddy Moreton *(Artist)*,*Charlton Musgrove, Somerset*

Ingredients:

3 eggs
4 oz flour
1 orange — finely grated rind then squeezed
4 oz granulated sugar
1 oz butter

Method:

Set oven to 190C/375F/Gas Mark 5. Beat the eggs and the sugar together in a warmed bowl (this works better if both are a little warm). Mixture should become thick, pale and mousse-like quite quickly. Into the bowl sieve the flour with a pinch of salt. Gently pour in the heated juice of the orange in which the butter has been melted; add the finely grated rind (no white pith). Fold together as lightly as possible but persevere until it is thoroughly mixed. Spoon into two 7-inch sandwich tins and bake for about 20 minutes until springy. When cool sandwich together with orange-flavoured whipped cream, or marmalade for grown-ups, and dust with caster sugar.

Comment: Very moist and very delicious.

QUEEN ELIZABETH THE QUEEN MOTHER'S FAVOURITE CAKE

Mrs Therese Juxon, *Tunbridge Wells*

Ingredients:

4 oz dates, chopped
6 oz sugar
6 oz sifted plain flour
1 egg, beaten
1 tsp baking powder
1 tsp bicarbonate of soda
2 oz butter
2 oz walnuts, chopped
1 tsp vanilla essence
½ tsp salt

Topping:

5 tbsp soft light brown sugar
2 tbsp cream (top of milk)
2 tbsp butter

Method:

Line a swiss roll tin with foil building it up well at the sides (about 9″ x 12″ tin). Pour a cup of boiling water over chopped dates and bicarbonate of soda. Let it stand, mix the cake ingredients, leaving a few chopped walnuts for topping, and then add to date mixture, stirring well. Bake for 35 minutes in a moderate oven.

Topping: Mix together topping ingredients and boil for 3 minutes. Spread over cake and top with chopped nuts.

Comment: This is the Queen Mother's favourite cake recipe. At her request, it must **not** be given but **sold,** and the money donated to a charitable organisation.

INDEX

		Page
STARTERS:	Italian Antipasta	8
	Basil & Tomato Soufflé	9
	Chalet Cheese & Mushroom Soufflé	10
	Chicken Liver Pâté	11
	Insalata Del Fungi	12
	Layered Sardine Pâté	13
	Magic Mushrooms	14
	Pâté En Croute	15
	Smoked Salmon and Noodles	16
	Hot Spinach Cheesecake	17
SOUPS:	Artichoke Soup	20
	Iced Carrot and Orange Soup	20
	Leek and Potato Soup	21
	Lentil Souperb	22
	Quick Onion Soup	23
	Stilton and Vegetable Soup	24
	Pam's Tomato Soup	25
	Tuscan Bean Soup	26
	Watercress Soup	27
FISH:	Fish Steak Casserole	30
	Haddock Monte Carlo	31
	Prawn Bhoona	32
	Salmon Steaks with Avocado Butter	33
	Spicy Prawns with Couscous Salad	34
BEEF:	Fillet Steak Royale	36
	Italian Spaghetti Sauce	37
	Veal Medallions with Asparagus tips, Lobster and Hollandaise	38
CHICKEN:	Buffalo Wings	39
	Chicken in an Apricot & Ginger Sauce	40
	Chicken Breasts with Cream Cheese & Wrapped in Parma Ham	41
	Chicken with Mint & Avocado	42
	Chicken & Stilton Bombs	43
	Easy Chicken Divan	44
	Lemon Chicken	45
	Mango & Mustard Chicken	46
	Oriental Chicken with Noodles	47
	Raspberry Chicken	48
	Thai Chicken Curry	49

		Page
GAME:	Roast Duck with Cherry Sauce	50
	Duck a l'Orange	51
	Pheasant Pot–Roast	52
	Pheasant Salad	53
	Roast Pheasant with Whisky & Raisins	54
LAMB:	Fillet of Lamb Casserole	55
	Stuffed Loin of Lamb	56
	Lamb with Apricots	57
LIVER:	Stir Fry Liver	58
	Tranche of Calf's Liver, Sauce Bercy	59
PASTA:	Lamb & Cheesy Pasta Casserole	60
	My Pasta	61
	Pasta with Rosemary & Chilli	62
	Pasticcio Di Rigatoni E Pollo	63
	Prawn & Pasta Salad	64
	Spicy Pasta	65
PORK:	Bacon Risotto	66
	Chinese Pork Fillet	67
	Ham Rolls from the Piddle Valley	68
	Pork Escalopes with Ginger & Cream	69
	Pork & Prunes	69
	Veal or Pork Maintenon	70
VEGETARIAN:	Aubergine, Tomato & Red Pepper Terrine	72
	Caronata	73
	Grilled Mediterranean Vegetables	74
	Italian Baked Asparagus	75
	Little Mushroom Pies	76
	Marinated Mushrooms	77
	Mushroom Roast	78
	Potato Cakes	79
	Potato Gratin-Provencal Version	80
	Savoury Nut Roast	81
	Scalloped Potatoes	82
THIS & THAT:	Cheese on Toast	84
	Chocolate Sauce	85
	Crab Savoury	85
	Fudge	86
	Meat Loaf	87
	Pear Chutney	87
	Some Kind of Salad	88
	Stem Ginger Truffles	89
	Stilton & Sesame Biscuits	89
	Thunder & Lightning	90
	Tinned Delight	91
	Wonderful Orange Sauce	91

		Page
PUDDINGS:	Abbotts Barton (Raspberries)	94
	Apple Tart with a Calvados Sabayon	95
	Banoffi Pie	96
	Boozy Bananas	97
	Caramel Peaches a la Pike	98
	Cherry Soup	99
	Chocy Meringue Pudding	100
	Chocolate Mousse Alla Romana	101
	Creme Brulee, Pommes Sec, Jus de Granny Smith	102
	Plop Pudding	103
	Rhubarb Fudge Crumble	104
	Roast Figs	105
	Scrumptious White Chocolate Cheesecake (uncooked)	106
	Seattle, USA Cheesecake	107
	Zebra Cake	108
ICE CREAMS:	After Eight Ice Cream	110
	Blackberry Ice Cream	110
	Crunchie Bar Ice Cream	111
	Lemon & Orange Ice Cream	111
	Rhubarb & Ginger Sorbet	112
	Strawberry Ice Cream	112
CAKES:	Banana Cake	114
	Boiled Fruit Cake	114
	Carrot Cake	115
	Chocolate & Orange Cake	116
	Chocolate Cake	117
	Crunch	118
	Date & Walnut Loaf	119
	Double Chocolate Chip Brownies	120
	Fat Girls Fudge Cake	121
	Kempton Cookies	122
	Nutty Gooey Topping Cake	122
	Millionaires Shortbread	123
	Orange Butter Sponge	124
	Queen Elizabeth The Queen Mum's Cake	125